Misfit Spirit

Reflections and Remarks
of a Religion Rebel

Jay Sakashita

ISBN-13: 978-0-9971305-9-1
Library of Congress Control Number: 2018947511

Tree drawings by Skye and Stirling Sakashita
First Printing, October 2018

Produced by:
Mutual Publishing, LLC
1215 Center Street, Suite 210
Honolulu, Hawai'i 96816
Ph: (808) 732-1709
Fax: (808) 734-4094
e-mail: info@mutualpublishing.com
www.mutualpublishing.com

Printed in South Korea

Contents

Introduction & Acknowledgments

Apassage from the Quran (22:47) states a thousand years is like a day to God. This is Tamagotchi time. By this reckoning, I may have been teaching religion classes at the University of Hawai'i since 1998 and writing my religion column for *MidWeek* newspaper since 2014, but in God days I've been doing both for a mere 36 minutes.

Time flies when you're having fun, though I've found it moves at different speeds when writing a religion column. My heart rate too, fluctuates from the rapid beat at the anticipation of seeing my article in print, to suddenly pausing as I read the less than complimentary responses to my articles from readers. And yet I do it again and again. There is an endless cycle of death and rebirth in Hinduism called *samsara*, and it seems I've stumbled into the publishing equivalent: writing, publishing, regretting, writing…

The first person the Buddha met after his enlightenment shook his head and walked away unimpressed. Though far from anything enlightened, the articles in this collection have met with similar reactions from readers and perhaps even worse. I've received numerous complaints, criticism, and taunts. Many were quite nasty and some even came from people not in my family.

In my view, there is no one true way. The Dao—like water—takes many forms. In religion, people search for patterns and meanings when sometimes none exist. All faiths flow from this search. There are strengths and weaknesses in religion, each transforming into the other at times, and the articles in this book try to ponder both.

Confucianism values the family and social harmony. I am very lucky to have a team of family members that previews my writings before I submit them for publication—a sister with traditional values, another with a liberal point of view, a daughter who happily points out my flaws, a mom who thought she was Christian, my wife who claims to be Buddhist, and my dad and my son and my de facto brother-in-law (who simply listen to what the women in the family tell them)—to warn me when they find anything offensive, in poor taste, or threatens the Confucian principle. I should listen to their advice.

An angry email accused me of blasphemy for distorting the Bible and misleading people. This came from a member of one of the churches charged in a lawsuit several years ago with cheating public schools out of millions of dollars in rental fees. The pot can still call the kettle black, I guess. Another reader sent an anonymous, rambling, 5-page hand-scribbled letter to the university religion department, demanding that I apologize for "denigrating" Buddhism. At first I thought it was a joke, because a few changes here and there and it would have made for a model ransom note. A similar letter followed a couple of weeks later. I sometimes wish Jesus did not make the number of times we are to forgive each other so high. (Matthew 18:22)

Gratitude is stressed in Shinto and I must emphasize here that not all responses have been negative. Many were quite complimentary and encouraging. For these I am grateful. I consider it a privilege to write for *MidWeek* and I am indebted to Ron Nagasawa, Don Chapman and Terri Hefner for the opportunity they gave me to create my *Misfit Spirit* religion column. I am grateful to Jane Gillespie at Mutual Publishing too, for her patience and kindness in helping my articles take book form. And I am thankful for the wonderful opportunity to work with such good people in the arts & humanities division at Leeward Community College and in the religion department at the University of Hawai'i at Mānoa. Friedrich Seifert, George Tanabe and Ian Reader were professors of mine and teaching messiahs who inspired me to be curious and helped me see religion from all points of view, even from those not necessarily popular or comfortable. I am especially grateful to my students for asking questions that are both inspiring and irritating. Many of my articles began as responses to their questions. My family and friends in Singapore too, support me with their kindness and help me to see things from a different perspective. In Hawai'i, Blythe, Shari and Jonathan asked that I not mention their names—so I won't. Most of all, I am thankful for my wife Pauline, daughter Skye, and son Stirling. I love them with everything that I am.

One of the things I've learned from writing about religion is that the issues and themes I can discuss in a college course do not translate well in a 700-word column. In fact, it often times fails miserably and people get angry with me as a result. As I usually do, I turned to scripture for guidance. I found Psalms 86:17 in the Bible: *Show me a sign of your favor, so that those who hate me may see it and be put to shame, because you, God, have helped me and comforted me.*

It was then that an overseas lawyer emailed me with information about a wealthy client who died and left me a vast amount of money. Almost immediately afterwards, a woman from Nigeria emailed me about funds floating in her country's central bank that she wished to transfer to me. I only had to let her know my bank account number. And to top it all off, a Miss Nadia, a Miss Sonia, and a guy named Hank began sending me weekly emails telling me we were meant to be partners in love. I am to send money and photos. God truly works in mysterious ways.

I dedicate this book to my dad, Stanley Sakashita, and to the memory of my mom, Barbara Sakashita. My mom passed away on February 23, 2016. She used to save each newspaper article of mine, no matter how bad it was. My dad now continues the tradition. My dad does the best he can to live for my mom and for us. We miss her dearly. We are because of her.

I hope you enjoy the articles.

Reflections

Religion Labels

I get asked the same question every semester in class—"What is your religion?" My standard response is, "It depends on the day." Some days I need forgiveness, some days I need to be enlightened. Most days I need both.

I am nourished by different religions.

When my children were younger, they too would sometimes ask me, "What are we? Are we Christian, Buddhist, or what?" I told them, "Don't worry about labels. Be strong and kind and you'll be fine." It doesn't matter what others say. A strong spirit and kind heart works in every religion, regardless of the faith label.

Labels don't matter. Calling me rich will not add a single penny to my bank account. Likewise, calling someone Christian, Buddhist, religious, or an atheist does not suddenly change who that person is. Religious labels don't make one moral or dangerous. How a person lives and treats others does instead. But religion labels are convenient and we use them instead of thinking. Labels give us an excuse not to make an effort to understand what a person or religion really is like. But labels should be placed on food packages to tell us what's inside—not on people to tell others what they are.

While the labels themselves don't matter, the act of labeling a person does. Slapping religion labels on people limits who they are and places them in neat, prefabricated categories that feed stereotypes. Yes, labels can be a step towards eventual understanding, but often they are obstacles to it instead. Besides, religion nametags are rarely helpful.

Some of the most compassionate and accepting people are religious; and some of the most bigoted and hateful people are also religious. In fact, you can find both in the same religion. Labeling someone as religious is therefore meaningless. Consider Thich Nhat Hanh and Ashin Wirathu. One is a world-renowned peace activist, while the other is accused of inciting religious violence in Myanmar. Both do so in the name of Buddhism. To call them Buddhists tells us little about the men and even less about Buddhism.

Perhaps even more dubious than those who paste labels on others are those who stick labels on themselves. Those who convert to a religion often try to meet the expectations of their newfound faith and may lose themselves in the process. I can speak from experience. As a born-again Christian, I tried to share the gospel with everyone I met, including strangers and customers at my part-time job. I read the Bible everyday, listened to Christian talk radio and Christian music. I even tried to convert my religion professor. Wrong move. Several years later, as a Buddhist minister in training, I dedicated myself to the religion. I practiced meditation, but fell asleep; I tried chanting sutras, but only AC/DC lyrics filled my head. I quit trying to belong to either religion. Both religions belong to me instead.

Identifying with a particular religious tradition may be an essential component of a person's self-understanding, but it should not be the primary or most important one. Religions should support one's identity, not the other way around. There is little need to subsume one's identity for the sake of a religious label. Moreover, it's not necessary to have just one (or any) religion label.

I don't have to choose just one identity, but can hold several simultaneously. For example, I can be male, American, Japanese, kamaʻaina, and sexy all at once. So too, I can (and do) hold Christian values, Buddhist ideals, Shinto sensitivities and Confucian principles—among others—at the same time. I take what I like about the existing religions and discard what I don't. I consider this spiritual crossfit training and I am religiously healthier and stronger because of it. I don't fit neatly or completely into any one particular religion box. I'm a misfit spirit. Many others are probably the same way. We can take comfort that Jesus, Muhammad, the Buddha and the other religious greats also did not fall nicely under one label and were criticized by the religion establishment of their day as a result.

When it comes to engaging in meaningful dialogue to understand the religion identity of others, then, the only label that should be used is the one similar to the directions on food stuff in my cupboard: tear to open.

Autumn Of My Life

The seasonal calendar mirrors my personal calendar at the moment. I am in the autumn of my life. Knowing this, the fall season feels a little different for me this year. I don't see autumn as simply a prelude to the winter holiday season anymore. And what is more, I am mindful that the number of good autumns I have left is dwindling. As a result, my awareness of the fall season is keener this year than in years past. I am not anxiously looking ahead nor am I longing to go back. I am happy to linger where I am for a while to look at the changing world around me and reflect on the shifting world within me.

"For everything there is a season,
and a time for every matter under heaven."
–Ecclesiastes

I was lucky to experience the autumn season in Scotland and Japan when I lived in those countries during my days as a graduate student. I remember being in awe of the brilliant yellow, orange and red foliage on the trees, as I had never seen such things before. I enjoyed the feeling of the crunching sensation under my feet too, as I stepped on the fallen leaves as I walked to and from school. And I felt reflective whenever I saw one of the leaves from a tree float to the ground. It was a clear reminder of the fleeting nature of the moment and that everything has its own time.

"God is concealed in every heart"
–Guru Nanak

I later learned that the leaves didn't actually turn yellow, orange, or red. Those colors were always there; they were simply hidden under the green. The leaves were green because of the chlorophyll, a key ingredient that helps feed the tree and color its leaves. In the autumn, however, with the lessening amounts of warmth and sunshine, the chlorophyll breaks down and the green gives way to the colors that were there all along—the magical reds, golds, and oranges of the fall. The leaves in turn can draw out the sense of wonder, beauty, and awe that dwell within us all.

"Out of nowhere the mind comes forth."
–Diamond Sutra

Like chlorophyll, the desires and needs that motivated me in the past and colored my world have begun to break down in the autumn of my life. Those ambitions served me well when I was younger and I got an education, a job, and a god as a result (though not in that order). I no longer solely value my life based on my college degree, work, or faith, however. They are still important to me, but I get more contentment and fulfillment from other places in my life now. I don't know from where or when I realized this, but the most wonderful things in life can also be found in the most simple things in life.

"Who is rich? Those who rejoice in their own lot."
—Talmudic Proverb

Nothing is more valuable or important to me than family. Some people tell me, however, that they put their god first before their family. I suggest they change gods or get a better family. The preciousness of family has been made all the more clear to me because too many of the leaves from my family tree have fallen in recent years. And despite my best efforts, the changing color of my hair tells me that the time for my leaf to flutter to the ground is gradually approaching. Yet the leaves that have fallen nourish the soil that feeds the tree. They will help bring about a beauty and a spring I cannot yet see. I am grateful for the richness of the leaves.

"God will not change the condition of a people until they change what is in themselves."
–Quran

Whether through study or practice, religion has been a part of my whole adult life. When I was younger, I tended to see everything through the color of religion. I read, heard, or recited a wide variety of prayers from the different religious traditions. But if I had to choose just one prayer to sustain me for the rest of my life, I would side with Meister Eckhart, the Christian thinker and mystic who said, "'Thank you' is the only prayer necessary." How fitting then, in this season of giving thanks that I am grateful for the leaves of religion that have brought me warmth and sunshine (and darkness and despair) as I watch them fall away in the autumn of my life.

Buddhist Valentine

Next week, my wife and I will spend yet another Valentine's Day together. I've run out of ideas of affordable things to get her for a gift. Why must we buy something new every year? One Valentine's Day gift should be enough to last a lifetime. But because of Buddhism, I've learned that nothing lasts, all is impermanent, and everything changes. Things change in a marriage over the course of 19 years too. In the beginning of our relationship, my love for my wife was such that I couldn't imagine life without her and I wanted us to be together forever. Now...I hope my wife dies first.

Buddhism is responsible for this change in attitude.

Most Buddhists in the world do not get married at a Buddhist temple. This is a shame, but it's understandable. After all, no one really wants to be standing at the altar with the love of your life on this most joyous day and have a Buddhist priest tell you, "Nothing lasts. Life is suffering."

And yet, this should be the very message that is conveyed to all married couples on their wedding day—for if a marriage is to be successful, the couple must be willing to accept change and appreciate change through the good times and bad. This is true not just for marriages, but for any kind of relationship, including those celebrated on Valentine's Day.

Perhaps the most serious threat to a long-term relationship is the temptation for one person to take the other person for granted. This is more likely to happen if you believe nothing changes and love lasts forever. Things do change and love doesn't stay the same (it moves and shifts). When changes come—and they inevitably will—clinging to past notions of what a person was like or to the feelings one used to have will bring pain.

The Sigalovada Sutta contains the teachings of the Buddha to a young householder regarding the various relationships we have in our lives. The Buddha instructs Sigala that happiness can be found by fulfilling our responsibilities to others. During their conversation, the Buddha offers common-sense advice to married couples too. Here are three:

Be attentive and kind to each other.

In 1988, the American pop group Exposé had a #1 hit song, *Seasons Change*. This might as well have been a Buddhist anthem, for a recurring line in the chorus tells us, "Seasons change. Feelings change...People change." Relationships can be lost when we are not attentive to the other person and don't value the changes over time, however subtle, that occur within our loved ones and us.

Be faithful to each other.

Changes can spark a renewed commitment to the other person. Many couples renew their wedding vows years after first getting married. It is a celebration of their commitment to one another through the changes. My parents renewed their marriage vows on their 50th wedding anniversary. Yet one doesn't need to wait 50 years or even be married to affirm a promise to be true to another person. With each change comes the opportunity to uphold the pledge to honor each other.

Share responsibilities and take care of each other.

The conditions and circumstances that created the occasion for a relationship to first develop and flourish will fade away. New ones will arise, however, that provide opportunities to work together and help each other. One cannot simply rely on the feelings and attitudes of the past to sustain the present. Supporting each other when facing difficult situations and leaning on one another when meeting new challenges can reinvigorate a relationship.

Before the Exposé song closes, the band wails, "I'll sacrifice tomorrow. Just to have you here today."

The deep sorrow that will arrive in the days after a loved one is gone is worth the price to pay for the wonderful relationship we share with that person now. How lucky we are to have people in our lives whose absence brings us sadness. Let us enjoy the company of loved ones while there is the opportunity to do so, for things will change. Buddhism teaches that every one of our relationships will come to an end—either due to separation or death. I've witnessed the pain, emptiness and confusion in the person who has lost a spouse. I've pondered the possible scenarios for my wife and me and I've decided that I want to protect my wife from the overwhelming grief that accompanies the days of loss and loneliness for the one left behind. Therefore, for this Valentine's Day I will tell her, "I love you so much. I hope you die first."

We Are Stars

Winter solstice is a pivotal point on the calendar. It is the longest night of the year (in the northern hemisphere), which means after this night the power of light begins to reassert itself. The skies above signal to the earth below that the season of cold and darkness must soon give way to a period of warmth and renewal. Accordingly, many peoples and many cultures mark this time of the year with festivals and holidays that celebrate the power of light over darkness. Hanukkah (the Jewish festival of light), Christmas (the Christian celebration of the birth of Jesus, who is called the light of the world), and Bodhi Day (the Buddhist holiday that marks the occasion when Siddhartha Gautama achieved enlightenment) all share in this common theme.

People in antiquity may have concluded that the sun was weakening—even dying—during the approaching winter as they observed the world around them get darker and colder. Perhaps the world within them too, experienced a similar change. And without light and warmth, there can be no life. Even so, a collection of brilliant stars known as the Winter Circle is visible in the night sky. It is no coincidence then, that symbols of abundance and wishes of good fortune were valued during a time of scarcity and uncertainty. They are expressions of the affirmation of life.

Religions too, looked to the lights in the night sky for celestial guidance and created stories about messages the stars conveyed regarding who we are and what we mean.

According to the Gospel of Matthew, a star rose above Bethlehem to mark the birth of Jesus and led the wise men to the house where Mary and her child were. According to the Buddhist tradition, after overcoming the various temptations of Mara (the personification of evil), Siddhartha Gautama achieved enlightenment when he saw the rise of the morning star. And although the Star of David is a fairly recent creation in the history of Judaism, one tradition traces the origin of the interlocking triangle symbol to a prophet and seer in the Bible—Balaam, a man with a talking donkey—who foretold the coming of a star that would emerge out of Israel.

Lights also cast dark shadows, however. The birth of Christ the Savior would bring about the killing of children two years old and younger. Mara would persist in antagonizing the Buddha, eventually playing a role in preventing the Enlightened One from living longer than he did. And Balaam also caused God's people to turn away from God, resulting in a deadly plague that killed 24,000 people. The plague was stopped when the bodies of those who turned away from God were impaled in the sun.

In religion and elsewhere, we view the stars with awe. Whether we try to understand the stars in seriousness (astronomy) or interpret them through silliness (astrology), the stars hold an attraction to us. They help us comprehend the universe around us and make sense of the world within us. We have an affinity for the stars for they are like us: they are born, live for a period of time, and die. What is more, we live because stars have died. We are its remnants.

We live in the universe and in a very real sense the universe exists within us. Indeed, the ingredients that make up the stuff in our bodies were created billions of years ago by cosmic explosions. As astrophysicist Carl Sagan famously said, "We're made of star stuff." In fact, the top five elements in the universe—hydrogen, helium, oxygen, carbon, nitrogen—parallel the most common ingredients in our bodies, with the exception of helium. (We don't have helium in our bodies, yet we are strangely attracted to it, especially when we want to make our voices sound silly.)

Science tells us we are a collection of stardust; religions say we carry its light. In the Gospel of Matthew, for example, Jesus tells his followers that they are lights of the world. In a translation of the Mahaparinibbana Sutta, the Buddha encourages his disciples to be lamps and to seek refuge in its light. And the prophet Isaiah informs God's people that God has given them as a light to the nations.

The light of some of the stars closest to us began during the time of the dinosaurs and only reaches us now. Some of those stars no longer exist. And yet the lights from the stars generated long ago aid modern day astronomers in calculating the structure of the universe and in predicting its direction. From starlight we can discern what came before and what is yet to come. Everything is in the stars.

Light and darkness come from the same sky and faith. The past, present, and future can be found in the stars and dwell in each of our bodies. Winter solstice, then, heralds the arrival of a new year—a passageway between a part of us that is 13 billion years old and another part of us that is yet to be born.

Ode To Music And Religion

Two days before Christmas in 1985, two young men made a suicidal pact to end their lives
    Walked to a Nevada church playground so they could be found dead, both took shotguns and shot themselves in the head
One died instantly on that fateful day, the other suffered for three more years with his face nearly blown away
Drugs, alcohol, and the music of Judas Priest,
Caused the two to kill themselves, is what their parents believed

A lawsuit and a trial followed that gripped enemies and friends
Until a judge ruled that Judas Priest was not liable for the deaths of the two men

Religion is like Music
It is raw and refined. It is sordid and sublime.
Faith is a song if you listen to it
See what you can find. Unearth what's in your mind.

Paris, January 7, 2015, two men attacked the headquarters of Charlie Hebdo, a satirical magazine
Drove to the newspaper to silence the product it issued each week that blasphemed their holy faith through its practice of free speech
They donned black masks and stormed into the room, and demanded by name those who penned offensive cartoons
Gunfire from Kalashnikov rifles shattered the calm
As two brothers killed 12 people in the name of Islam

The link between religion and violence, people continue to debate
But scholars know religion does not cause love or episodes of hate

Islam is like Judas Priest
Something for the strong; something for the weak
Emotions and passions are tamed and unleashed
A mixture of the beautiful with a dose of the bleak

Religion and music are canvases that lay bare the subtle palette of emotions
* already there*
Music and religion are not the cause of grace and hate, but reflections and
* expressions of what they create*
The fear, hope and hurt within will lead us to salvation or drive us deeper
* into sin*
What is festering inside or blooming therein, explains why some people turn
* to music and others find religion*

Only praised or blamed—but rarely understood—that's not how it should be
Religion like Music must be enjoyed responsibly

Rob Halford and Muhammad
The voice of heavy metal; the messenger of God
Calling out the faithful; beckoning the flawed
Not a poet, nor a prophet; I will keep to my day job

Gold & Gods

When I walk into the local Buddhist temples and see the array of gilded items on the altar area, the first thing that comes to my mind is the pawnshop. Yes, that place that sells gently worn, pre-owned jewelry. Actually, I don't only associate pawnshops with Buddhist temples. I think of inexpensive jewelry during Christmas, Birthdays, Valentines Day, and anniversaries as well.

What is it about cheap jewelry that attracts me? The price. I find it intriguing how anyone can attach a price tag to a piece of metal, precious or otherwise. For example, several weeks ago gold was selling at $1364/oz. When I heard the exciting news I quickly went to the back of my closet, where I keep a shoebox hidden—away from moths, away from dust (away from my wife)—that holds the letters from a former girlfriend. And there tucked beneath the stack of notes and envelopes is a gold ring that my former girlfriend gave me in 1984. And because I now have two children whose combined school tuition is $45,000 a year—I could use $1364/oz! So I put the gold ring in my pocket and headed out the door to the pawn-shop, but something didn't feel right. Something inside me said, "Wait… Wait until it's $1400/oz!" No, I couldn't sell the gold ring because it had taken on a different value for me over the years.

Throughout history gold has been valued in different cultures and among different religions for similar reasons. First of all, gold is incorruptible: it is resistant to chemical reactions and immune to the corrosion that affects baser metals. It has a lasting quality and embodies strength and consistency as a result. Secondly, gold is intrinsically luminous, seeming to shine with a light all its own. Gold thus symbolizes purity, perfection and immortality.

Due to these associations, gold is often linked to the sacred. Hindu and Daoist texts identify gold with immortality. The Christian Bible describes heaven with streets of gold. The Torah depicts the mercy seat of God in the Ark of the Covenant as pure gold. The Quran states doers of righteousness will be rewarded with gold. And in Buddhism, buddhas are frequently portrayed in gold.

Despite its symbol as a source of strength and stability, gold is also a soft metal. Gold is malleable and can be fashioned into something even more wonderful. In short, gold is lasting and changing at the same time.

What is truly attractive about the assortment of used jewelry in pawn-shops is that each piece of jewelry has seen some of the changes in some of the people's worlds. Each piece comes from a different place and brings a different story and it has the potential to be a part of someone else's story—someone else's world.

When our daughter was a little girl, she would say to my wife, "Mommy, can I have your gold bracelet when you die?" We laughed and thought how cute she was to ask, but we made a mental note to sleep with one eye open just in case she decided to hasten the event. My wife told her that she would pass along the bracelet to her as an heirloom on her graduation day. That day is now just around the corner. Over the years, that bracelet has witnessed a lot of our happy times and heartaches. My daughter will enrich and deepen the bracelet with her own story and render it even more valuable.

We all come from different backgrounds and we bring different stories. And during this time of the year we meld our backgrounds and stories as we share meals and the company of others in gratitude and thanksgiving.

Some years I have a lot to be thankful for. This year not so much. While there is a fair amount of pain, loss, and suffering every year, this year has been especially heartbreaking for my family—my mom died. But just as gold flakes may emerge by chance from broken rocks, sometimes a heart breaks in the right way and for this I am thankful. From pain we find our own strength and beauty, from suffering we gain a keener sense of compassion, and from loss we learn understanding and acceptance. When you've lost someone dear, suffering and joy come from the same place. Now my sadness is my strength; my sorrow is my smile.

Not only are buddhas made of gold, but other symbols in Buddhism as well. According to what is known as the *Contemplation Sutra,* a golden lotus welcomes one to the Pure Land of Amida Buddha. What is the significance of the lotus blossom in Buddhism? The lotus grows in a pond of mud and stagnant water. Yet from the muck a beautiful blossom emerges. If there is no mud, there can be no lotus.

Religions thus preach not only salvation *from* suffering, but also salvation *through* suffering.

Just as a cataclysmic event in the universe (the smashup of neutron stars) produced glimmering riches of dust that transformed into gold, religions preach that pain, loss, and suffering can be transformed into compassion, gratitude and forgiveness. In fact, there is a Buddhist prayer that says, "May I be given the appropriate difficulties so that my heart can truly open with compassion. "

So as we enter the holiday season, I offer this prayer: May your families be well, your hearts and minds at peace, and that the rest of this year and the next be rich and rewarding and as valuable as gold, and something that you will be thankful for and cherish for a long, long time—or at least until it hits $1400/oz.

Beauty In Something Ugly

I don't have much. But of all the things that I do own, one stands out—a homemade doll. It consists of little more than part of a cut-off pajama pant leg, stuffed with tissue and—so that the stuffing won't fall out—tied tightly on the top and bottom with masking tape. In fact, a big piece of masking tape is stuck on the upper portion of the figurine and a face is drawn on it with a ballpoint pen. My son made this for me and gave it to me as a gift several years ago. When he showed it to me, my first thought was, "He needs art lessons." After getting over the initial shock, though, I've come to appreciate the doll. It is horrifically beautiful. I wouldn't trade it for the most expensive doll in the world or any religious figurine, no mater how fancy or blessed it may be. I'll keep my deformed doll. I never thought I could love something so ugly.

My precious doll sits on the windowsill in our kitchen staring at me. It reminds me how quickly time passes and how fast children grow. It also reminds me that sometimes the giver of a gift is more important than the gift itself. This is especially important for me to keep in mind during this time of the year, when it is easy to value what is given more than the person behind the giving.

The various world religions teach that we are shaped by our relationships. And in turn our relationships are shaped through gifts. The gods give us gifts—their teachings, forgiveness, and grace; and we reciprocate with gifts of our own—tithing, faith, and ourselves.

Gifts can heal and make relationships whole. The apostle Paul, writing to members of a divided church, said the greatest of all the gifts is love—putting the needs of others before one's own and caring for others without regard for one's own standing. The prophet Muhammad said: "Exchange gifts, as this will strengthen your love for one another." The apostle and the prophet were right.

We give gifts to enrich and strengthen our relationships and make others happy. Gifts are more than just material items. They are tangible expressions we make to one another about the role we play in each other's lives.

But there is enough emphasis on giving during this time of the year. There should be more of a focus on receiving. Muhammad said that no one should look down upon a gift, no matter what the gift is. All gifts received should be appreciated. After all, giving and receiving are two sides of the same coin. They are the yin and yang of relationships, for there can be no giving without receiving and no receiving without giving. One flows into the other and back again. This is illustrated in the yin-yang symbol itself.

The Chinese cosmological concept of the "Great Ultimate" is a familiar symbol to many of us. It consists of a circle divided into two tear-drop-shaped halves—one white and the other black. And contained within each half is a dot of the other color. The dark half is yin and the light half is yang. When yin reaches a certain point it become yang and vice versa. At the height of yin there is a drop of yang and at the height of yang there is a spot of yin. From this point of view, the interaction of yin and yang gives birth to the fullness of life. The flow between giving and receiving fulfills us in our relationships.

My doll has taught me how to receive. From it I learned that not only do we receive when we give; we also give when we receive. We give appreciation for the other person when we receive with gratitude. We let the other person know how much they mean to us when we gratefully accept what is given.

And so I resisted the temptation to say to my son things that I would have said to others in the past when receiving gifts, such as: "I don't need anything," "You shouldn't have," or "You spent too much." Such phrases, though said with good intentions (I didn't wish to burden the person), essentially shut the giving person out from being a part of our lives. Instead, I said to my son, "Thank you. I like it very much!" I got a smile in return—a second gift from the same present. The yin was transformed into yang and back again. As I enjoyed the change and exchange, I marveled at how the beauty of a gift could be found in the ugliness of a doll.

Remarks

Teaching Religion

I enjoy teaching college-level religion courses. So much so in fact, that I'd do it for free.

Kidding aside, religion is a fascinating subject of study. People do incredible things—and incredibly stupid things—in the name of religion. Religion is there at the beginning of life (some claim they are born again because of it) and it is there at life's end (some die because of their faith). Religion helps mark the important transitions and events in our lives. And in my view, religion is the ideal major for college undergraduates. Through the study of religion, one is introduced to history, politics, science, art, literature, psychology and a host of other wonderful study subjects. In short, religion plays a vital role in helping us understand the world around us and also the world within us. I find it rewarding to help students learn, respect and appreciate the various religious traditions, especially in regards to religions different from their own.

But it is difficult to see objectively when perceptions are skewed by biases and preconceived notions, thus one of my tasks for the world religions course is to dispel misconceptions about religion. These misunderstandings present obstacles to the course goals of learning and tolerance. I first began teaching religion courses at the University of Hawai'i in 1998, and over the years I've noticed three commonly held misconceptions about religion that students tend to bring with them to class.

The first misunderstanding is the belief that each religion has only one true form. This is nonsense. The simple fact is there is no such entity as Christianity, Islam, or Buddhism. There are Christianities, Islams, and Buddhisms instead. Religions are internally diverse as each religion is characterized by a wide variety of beliefs and practices, some of which are seemingly contradictory. How many Buddhas are there? Who was Muhammad's rightful successor? Did Jesus preach an open acceptance of sinners or a moral standard that was non-negotiable? There are profound disagreements and debates within each of the religious traditions regarding such questions as Buddhists, Muslims, and Christians do not agree on a single answer. Therefore, it is always problematic to make sweeping claims about any religion and one must be especially wary of statements that begin with, "Muslims believe..." "Christians believe..." or "Buddhists believe..." Simply put, not all of them do.

A **second misunderstanding** is the belief that religions don't change. There is fluidity in religious identity as religions are not immune from interpretive shifts in history. What was considered Christian, Buddhist, or Hindu in the past may not be thought of in the same way today. Every religion has changed as believers interpret and reinterpret its message. Views of slavery, ethnicity, the role of women, and sexuality for example, have changed and continue to change within each tradition. Religious practice has changed too. Meditation was once a questionable practice at Hongwanji Buddhist temples because it focused on one's own efforts and could detract from relying on the saving power of Amida Buddha. Today meditation is promoted at the local Hongwanji temples.

The third misunderstanding about religion many students bring to class is the belief that religions function apart from their political, cultural, and economic contexts. Religions are not isolated from their environments, but interact with and are influenced by them. For example, I got married three times, each in a different religious tradition (my wife and I were trusting that at least one of the wedding rituals would be effective!). One of those weddings was held in a Christian church in the United Kingdom. Christianity in the United Kingdom is different from Christianity in the United States.

The concept known as "separation of church and state" is an official part of the U.S., but not in the U.K. Indeed, there is an established religion in England—the Church of England. What is more, the head of the Church of England is Queen Elizabeth II. There is no separation of church and state there. In the United States, by contrast, the government is prohibited from favoring or supporting one religious tradition over any other. Thus all religions are equal in the eyes of the law. As a result, religious groups in the United States must actively compete with each other to recruit potential followers to remain relevant. One is barely out the church door at some of the local Christian services before one is bombarded with

21

merchandise and sales pitches. This also explains the missionary emphasis of two of the most well-known religious groups that engage in door
to door preaching—Jehovah's Witnesses and Mormons. Both are Ameri-
can-born forms of Christianity.

Religions are collections of ideas, values, and practices that are inex-
tricably woven into our lives. Their various strands connect us to each
other and to the world around us. A better understanding of religion,
then, is crucial for meeting the variety of challenges and opportunities we
face today and into the future. Misconceptions about religion will prove
costly. Fortunately for those of us who teach religion, religious intolerance
persists and the illusion that there is a single, best, unchanging religion
is so widespread that we don't have to worry about doing what we enjoy
doing for free.

ON THE BIBLE

Creation Stories

Many Americans reject the scientific theory of evolution. They insist on a belief in creationism instead. What is more, they argue creationism should be presented alongside evolution in science classes and given equal time. This is nonsense. Yes, teachers should present different, even competing ideas to help build critical faculties among students, but not when experts in the field have debunked one of those ideas for its lack of merit.

At the University of Hawai'i, we don't teach astrology in astronomy; alchemy in chemistry; or flat earth theory in geology and geophysics. Outdated and irrational points of view have no place in serious academic settings. Yes, we offer a college course on *Witches & Witchcraft* and another called *Love, Sex & Religion* (which I don't teach because my wife says I only know a little about one of the three topics), but they are taught from a cross-cultural, historical point of view, and not as DIY classes.

Besides, if we were to teach creationism in our science classes, which creation story should we teach? There are so many. How about the Shinto version where the kami Izanagi and Izanami descended to earth over a heavenly bridge? Or the Hindu story of Purusha, who used his body parts to create society and the world? Since Buddhism is on the rise in America, how about the Buddhist creation story found in the *Agganna Sutta* that explains how gender, sexuality, private property, labor, and government came into existence? Creationists in America insist on the biblical account in the book of Genesis. Why? What makes the Genesis myth more acceptable than the others? And by the way, which Genesis creation story should we accept? There are two.

Many people do not know that there is more than one creation story in Genesis and are even less aware that the two creation stories in the Bible are incompatible and contradict each other. The two creation accounts in the Bible are: 1) the seven-day creation story (six days of creation and one day of rest) found in Genesis 1, and 2) the Adam & Eve story found in Genesis 2-3. Most people assume they are the same story from the same author and written from the same point of view. They are not. A detailed explanation of the differences between the two creation accounts is beyond the limits of this article, so I'll simply offer three pieces of evidence for readers to consider and pursue further on their own.

One, the order of creation: According to the seven-day account, God created humans on the sixth day, *after* God created plants and animals. According to the Adam & Eve story, however, man was created *before* plants and animals. In Genesis 1, the creation of humans is presented as God's culminating act. This explains why God gives us dominion over everything else. In Genesis 2-3, the creation of Adam is an incomplete act, which is why other things (animals and a woman) needed to be created to fill Adam's void.

Two, the name of God: According to the seven-day account in Genesis 1, God is referred to as *Elohim* (plural for God). According to the Adam & Eve story in Genesis 2-3, however, God is called *Yahweh* (translated as LORD). Moreover, *Elohim* is portrayed as distant and remote, an almighty creator who simply speaks and things come into existence. *Yahweh,* by contrast, is depicted here on earth and has human-like qualities—he works with dirt, walks in the garden in Eden, and isn't aware of everything (he doesn't know where Adam & Eve are hiding or what they've done). This suggests the different stories were produced from different sources with different concepts of God.

Three, the view of man and woman: According to Genesis 1, man and woman were created at the same time on the sixth day—both made in the image of God. They are equal. According to Genesis 2-3, however, Adam was created first and Eve was created from Adam's rib only after no suitable companion for Adam could be found among the animals. Thus Eve is not equal to Adam. She is subordinate to him, as *Yahweh* makes clear:

"your desire shall be for your husband, and he shall rule over you." (Genesis 3:16)

As an aside, there is a more positive view of the creation of humankind in Genesis 1 than there is in Genesis 2-3. After *Elohim* creates humans in Genesis 1, God tells them to be fruitful and declares things to be "very good." (Genesis 1:31) After *Yahweh* creates Adam in Genesis 2-3, by contrast, God tells him of a forbidden fruit and things go bad from there, ending with God expelling Adam and Eve from the garden of Eden and God placing an armed creature to prevent humans from access to the tree of life.

I love creation stories. Creation stories are religious myths—stories that may or may not be historically true, but convey profound truths. They have a place in understanding cultural values, as they are passageways to and expressions of the human spirit. As such, creation stories should not be taught in science classrooms, but in religion related courses where they belong. And they should be taught for what these stories are: purveyors of religious meaning, not repositories of scientific facts.

Burying The Dead

What do religions do with a dead body? Here in Hawai'i there are primarily two religious customs for dealing with the deceased: burn or bury. These options are usually tied to whether a religion teaches reincarnation or resurrection. In general, religious traditions that have notions of reincarnation cremate the dead and observe a series of memorial rites to facilitate the transformative process that moves the spirit of a loved one to the next stage of spiritual existence. Religions that believe in resurrection, however—Judaism, Christianity, and Islam—bury the dead.

There are two main reasons why Jews, Christians, and Muslims bury their dead. One, they believe in a bodily resurrection and cremation apparently renders this more difficult. Perhaps the clearest example of bodily resurrection comes from the Christian tradition, where the resurrected Christ appeared in a bodily form that could be seen and touched by his disciples. Due in part to this shared belief in bodily resurrection, enemies of Jews, Christians, and Muslims, have historically burned the bodies of the faithful to deny them the hoped-for afterlife. Cremation thus became a rejected practice in the three religious traditions, and even now some of the more conservative religious groups will deny a proper funeral for those choosing cremation or refuse to inter cremated remains in their cemeteries. It should be noted, however, that not all Jews, Christians, and Muslims in contemporary society view the issue of cremation in this way.

A second reason why burial is commonly practiced in Judaism, Christianity, and Islam is due to the fact that followers of all three religions worship the same god and believe in similar stories. The story of Adam and Eve and the Garden of Eden is one of these. According to the traditional account, Adam and Eve lost their innocence when, after a conversation with a serpent, Eve ate from the fruit of knowledge and also gave the fruit to Adam to eat. All three were punished as a result. The serpent lost its legs and potential kinship with humanity. The woman's punishment was pain during childbirth. As if that weren't enough, God added that as painful as childbirth would be, she would still desire it. There are sado-masochistic tones here, but this etiological story accounts for the fine line between pain and pleasure during childbirth. Though the serpent's punishment was harsh, and the woman's punishment cruel, the man's was worst of all: God punishes him because he listened to his wife (there's a not-so-subtle message in here for husbands) and ate the fruit. As punishment, Adam was sentenced to do yard work. This may seem benign, but the punishment is profound. The Hebrew word for ground is "adamah." Thus from "adamah" God created Adam. The English equivalent would be, from earth God fashioned earthling. The punishment, in other words, separates Adam from the source of his identity. The ground would no longer recognize Adam and produce for him. A part of him would be lost. Though he ate from the tree of knowledge, he will not know who he is, know where he came from, or know where he is headed. The story concludes with the man and woman cast out of the garden, and God arming angelic beings with flaming swords to guard its entrance and prevent humankind from turning back and eating from the tree of eternal life. God denies eternal life for Adam and Eve.

What happened to Adam and Eve? Adam and Eve traveled east of Eden where, according to Islam, the couple prayed to God for forgiveness and were forgiven. The couple's fate is not so clear in Judaism and Christianity. What is clear is the separation and alienation Adam and Eve experienced that would shape their fate. Herein lies the power of religion. The word "religion" literally means to "re-connect." When the body of the dead is buried then, the body is returned to the ground, identity is restored, and one is made whole again. In short, burying the body gives the dead life.

Cain & Abel

The famous story of Cain and Abel is found in the Bible (Genesis 4:1-17). Cain and Abel are the sons of Adam and Eve and they both make offerings to God. God accepts Abel's offering of a sacrificial lamb, but not Cain's offering of vegetables. In a fit of jealousy, Cain kills Abel. God discovers what Cain has done and curses him to roam as a wandering fugitive. God puts a mark on Cain to distinguish him from other people and sends him away.

If there is one conclusion to draw from the above story, it is this: vegetarians are dangerous.

Actually, the tale is more complex than that and cannot easily be deciphered. To begin with, it is clear that the story is NOT interested in answering certain questions contemporary readers may have: why did God accept Abel's offering but not Cain's? Couldn't God have accepted both? Perhaps God doesn't like vegetables (we are told in a later chapter that God loves the smell of roast meat). Cain is punished for killing

Abel, but how was he supposed to know this was a sin? God did not state murder was wrong until later in the Bible. Abel killed an animal, and God looked favorably upon this. Perhaps in the eyes of a vegetarian, this was an approval of murder. After Cain went out from God's sight, Cain and his wife produced a child. From where did Cain get his wife? There were only 4 (now 3) humans in existence at the time—Adam, Eve, Cain and Abel. The Bible simply doesn't care to answer these questions.

A key to deciphering the story may be to determine its literary genre. For example, if in the distant future one found a written document that read, "Ravens crush Cowboys" or "St. Francis beats St. Louis," one might think the animal kingdom rose up in a revolt against humankind or there was a holy war in heaven. Knowing instead that one has stumbled upon a newspaper sports page would provide a different interpretation.

Perhaps the Cain and Abel story is an etiology and not history. An etiology is a tale that tries to explain why things are the way they are. From this perspective, the Cain and Abel story may be trying to explain why shepherds and farmers don't get along, or why brothers fight.

Cain is the founder of the first city (Enoch). Perhaps the story is a reminder of why the city is so dangerous—a murderer founded it. Or it may be telling its readers that every homicide is actually a form of fratricide. There may be a moral component to the story too. Was Abel's sacrifice more fitting because he offered to God his best; while Cain simply gave what was available?

The potency of blood is an important theme in the Bible and it has its start here. The biblical God responds to blood: Abel's lamb's blood, Abel's blood (after he is murdered it calls out to God from the ground), covenantal blood (that Moses splashes on God's altar and on God's people), Jesus' blood.

What was the "mark of Cain" that God put on him? Was it something physical, psychological, or social?

The name Cain is related to the word "Kenite." In the Bible, the Kenites were loosely connected to the Israelites. Moses' father-in-law was a Kenite. The Kenites worshipped the same God as the Israelites and settled in the same land, but were not members of Israel. Perhaps the story is an explanation why the Israelites had an uneasy relationship with the Kenites. One had to know who they were and be careful with them, as they were connected to Cain, the one who killed his brother. Indeed, one of the best known murders in the Bible occurs when Jael, a Kenite woman, kills an enemy of the Israelites by luring him into her tent and then driving a tent peg into his head!

Even more disturbing, the mark of Cain has been misconstrued to justify racist beliefs. Although there is nothing in the story that indicates the mark was related to skin color, the idea that Cain was cursed with blackness—and that black people have inherited this curse—was used in the United States to justify slavery, support segregation, and exclude African Americans from church leadership.

Finally, where were the parents in this first family tragedy? Did Adam spare the rod with his murderous son? Perhaps he needed his Cane and he just wasn't Able. Ultimately like any good story, the tale of Cain and Abel is open to vast interpretations—revealing more about what's in our hearts and minds rather than what's in the story itself. For me, it's an urgent message to remind my son to be mindful of his vegetarian sister.

Misinterpretations That Emerged From Noah's Ark

The worst zoo I ever visited only had one dog in it—it was a Shih Tzu. The most incredible zoo, by contrast, must have been inside Noah's ark, where Noah and his family were confined with the entire animal kingdom for 150 days.

Understandably, after Noah emerged from his confinement, he planted a vineyard, drank some of the wine, became drunk, and lay uncovered in his tent. But (as Noah soon discovered) it's not good to pass out drunk and naked. His youngest son Ham—the father of Canaan—did something to Noah in this vulnerable state and then went outside to tell his brothers about what he had done. When Noah awoke from his drunken stupor and realized what Ham had done to him, Noah declared, "Cursed be Canaan; lowest of slaves shall he be to his brothers."

The events of this story were not only disturbing for Noah, but for anyone who tries to interpret this peculiar tale (Genesis 9). Three questions arise: what did Ham do to Noah; why did Noah curse Ham's son Canaan when it was Ham who committed the wrongful act; and why did Noah curse Canaan with slavery? Misinterpretations of this story have had tragic consequences.

Regarding the first question, Ham's offense must have been serious enough to warrant the punishment of eternal slavery. According to the biblical account, Ham saw the nakedness of his father. What does this mean and why was it so terrible?

The biblical writers were influenced by the beliefs and practices of the people around them; and their writings and stories reflect the influence of and interaction with these various outside traditions. Indeed the Noah story has parallels with other flood stories written centuries before the biblical account. An ancient document that may also have had an impact on the Noah story is known as the sex omens of Mesopotamia, which says the following:

"If a man repeatedly stares at his woman's vagina, his health will be good; he will lay his hands on whatever is not his. If a man is with a woman (and) while facing him she repeatedly stares at his penis, whatever he finds will not be secure in his house."

Seeing is an act of taking. The way one looks at another can be a form of aggression, dominance and control. To be the object of another person's stare makes one feel exposed and vulnerable. Thus Ham's looking at his father's nakedness may have been an attempt to dominate him.

Other scholars interpret Ham's offense as a physical form of sexual assault, perhaps sodomy or castration. This interpretation is based on the Hebrew words for *uncovered, saw,* and *nakedness;* which are used elsewhere in the Bible (Leviticus 18, Deuteronomy 20, Habakkuk 2) to detail perverse sexual acts, including incest. The name Ham, too, in Hebrew has connotations of sexual heat; and Sodom and Gomorrah were cities associated with Canaan. Moreover, the Mesopotamian writings referred to above also state that during male homosexual acts the active partner is accorded dominant status over his passive recipient.

Whatever the offense, the main issue seems to be power and control. In biblical times, the eldest son was entitled to his father's wealth, leaving the youngest son with virtually nothing. Ham, being the youngest of Noah's three sons, made a power play to assert his dominance over his older brothers. He did something to dominate Noah and then proceeded to inform his brothers what he had done, presumably to show them that he was now in the dominant position—the one in control. Noah responds with a curse of slavery, effectively removing Ham's claim of power and control.

In regards to the questions of why Noah cursed Ham's son Canaan when it was Ham who committed the wrongful act and why was the curse slavery, it is important to note that the Israelites considered Canaan as the land promised to them by God. The story of Noah and his sons was therefore used to justify the Israelites (descendants of Shem, Noah's oldest son) conquest and possession of the land occupied by the Canaanites (descendants of Canaan, son of Ham). In the view of the biblical writers, Canaanites were destined to be slaves in the land occupied by the Israelites.

It is always important to understand things in context, but this is especially so in regards to the Bible. The biblical stories were intended for particular people living in a particular place. They were not meant for people living centuries later in another continent. Unfortunately, the Noah story was taken out of context.

Genesis lists the descendants of Noah's sons and the nations associated with them. Ham's descendants include the peoples of North Africa. Ham's name would later be mistranslated to mean "black." The curse stemming from Ham's offense became interpreted as Africans bound to slavery. The belief that African-Americans were descendants of Ham was a primary justification for slavery among Southern Christians. The misconception that "blackness" was a curse resulted in the discrimination of blacks. Blacks were banned from leadership positions at some

Christian churches as a result, for example from the Mormon priesthood (since rescinded).

There are parts of the Noah story that can be applied to everyone everywhere, however. As I told my students prior to the revelry of the holiday season—it's just not a good idea to pass out drunk and naked, as it is not clear which side of the zoo cage the worst kinds of animals lie waiting.

Big Daddy Abraham

I go by different titles depending on who's calling me. The different designations indicate the different types of relationship I have with each person: "Daddy" (my children), "Professor" (my students), "Stud Muffin" (my wife, after three glasses of wine; "Idiot," without any alcohol). The same person would not address me substituting the different titles back and forth. That would be awkward, creepy or even illegal, depending on the combination of speaker and title.

Abraham is considered a patriarch in Judaism, Christianity, and Islam. Some even call Abraham the soul of the three monotheistic faiths. Yet Abraham goes by different titles in Judaism, Christianity, and Islam, reflecting the different understandings and assumptions each has of this seminal religious figure.

Abraham is referred to as Avraham Avinu (Our Father Abraham) in Judaism. He is considered the biological ancestor of the Jews and a biblical figure with whom God established an eternal covenant. God's promise to bless Abraham with children and land are intimately tied to this covenant. This explains in part why Judaism is linked to a particular ethnic identity—only children born to a Jewish parent are considered Jews (though ritual conversion is possible)—and why, according to the Bible, Israel refers both to a Chosen People and to a specific geographical location, the Promised Land. In Judaism, Abraham is viewed as a Torah observant fol-

32

lower of God, thus Jews take care to preserve and uphold the Torah as it is vital to maintaining their covenant with God.

Christians view Abraham as the "Father of Faith." In Christianity, one is not physically born into Abraham's family, but attains a spiritual birth in Abraham's lineage by embracing a similar faith and trust that Abraham had in God. Observing the Torah is of little consequence in this regard, which explains why Christians need not follow the biblical laws. Christians can break the 10 Commandments and still be saved, for if salvation came through the Torah then Jesus died for nothing. Faith in Christ trumps all sins. Abraham's faith was displayed in a required sacrifice that involved his only son. Ultimately a ram was sacrificed instead and God declared that blessings would come to Abraham and the world through him because of his trust in God. In Christianity, this episode foreshadowed the sacrifice of Jesus Christ, God's only begotten son, who is also called the Lamb of God. In Christianity, the covenant God established with Abraham is intimately tied to faith and the sacrifice of Jesus Christ.

Abraham has the title, Khalilullah (Friend of Allah) in Islam. He is "Father of the Prophets" (Ishmael, Isaac, Jacob, and culminating with the seal of the prophets—Muhammad). He is also referred to as Hanif (a person who is virtuous and devoutly obedient to God). Like Christianity, Islam is not tied to a particular ethnic lineage, but is open to anyone who actively seeks to obey the will of God. In the Quran, Abraham is an ardent monotheist who rejects the existence of other gods and vigorously destroys idols as a result. There is no equivalent story of this Abraham in the Bible. The Muslim view of Abraham underscores the clear prohibition of images of God in Islam. The emphasis on one God and no images in Islam is in stark contrast with the concept of the Holy Trinity and the use of images of Christ and icons of the Virgin Mary and the saints in Christianity.

Abraham cannot belong to all three religions. No one can. But he does belong to each religion. The Abraham of one religion differs profoundly from the Abraham in the others. In order for Abraham to belong to all three religions, one must change Abraham or change the religions that claim him. Neither is likely to happen, as it requires altering or even rejecting deeply cherished views of Torah, Christ, and/or the Quran.

Still, it may be worthwhile to consider the possibility of how different and even conflicting interpretations of Abraham may ultimately enrich our understanding of him. Reducing Abraham to a single narrative or insisting on only one interpretation of him, however, denies the complexity of his personality. It steals away from the richness of his character. It robs the soul of Abraham. And if we rob from the soul of Abraham, where does it leave the three world religions that claim Abraham has its soul?

Is Abraham one or three? The distinctive interpretations—expressed in the different names Jews, Christians, and Muslims call Abraham—prevent easy answers.

In short, names and titles tell us as much about the name-caller as they do about the one with the burden of carrying the name. Followers of Abraham may be calling me names as they read this. I hope they are finishing their third glass of wine as they do so.

A Lot On Lot

Finally, after a little more than ten years I can help my daughter with her homework again. The last time I was any good with her schoolwork was when she was in the second grade. I helped her with a math quiz. Not to boast, but I did pretty well. I scored 7 out of 10.

The first assignment for my daughter's college freshman English class was this: *Read the biblical story of Lot and discuss the ways in which it can be interpreted.* Easy. For me, the question might as well have been to write the answer to 10 + 1. (The answer is 11. Luckily, I'm a boy so I have more than my fingers to use for counting.)

First, a summary of the story. God decided to destroy the cities of Sodom and Gomorrah for their wickedness. Abraham argues with God and tries to persuade God from doing so. Later, two men—who are actually angels—travel to Sodom to visit the home of Abraham's nephew, Lot.

Lot offers them a lot, including food and lodging. Soon there is trouble, however. All the men of Sodom surround Lot's home and demand that Lot bring out his guests so that they can have sex with them. Lot begs the men not to treat his visitors in this way and offers the men his two virgin daughters instead, telling them that they can do to his daughters as they please. The men don't take Lot up on his offer and insist that Lot turn over his visitors to them. They try to break the house door down to get at Lot's two angel guests. The angels blind the men so that they cannot find the door and command Lot and his family to leave the city as God will destroy it. They also instruct Lot and his family not to look back at the city as they flee. Lot's wife does turn back to take a look (one tradition says she wanted to be sure her daughters were with them) and she is turned into a pillar of salt. Lot and his daughters escape and live in a cave in the mountains. Lot's daughters bemoan the fact that there is not a man left who can give them offspring. They devise a plan to get their father drunk and have sex with him on successive nights. They become pregnant and give birth to sons, who will become the ancestors of the Moabites and Ammonites. Lot had offered his daughters for rape; now his daughters rape him.

Why is such a story as this in the Bible? Students of mine are sometimes surprised to learn that there were no television sets, Internet, or phones during biblical times. "How did they watch movies?" They didn't. People in antiquity told stories instead--stories to entertain and stories to explain the world around them. The story of Lot ridiculed the Moabites and Ammonites, neighbors of the Israelites. The function of the story is similar to racist jokes I used to hear when I was in elementary school. It demeans other groups in order to bolster the standing of one's own.

The story has a moral aspect as well. Hosts were expected to provide hospitality and protection to strangers. The shameful behavior of the men of Sodom is condemned. The story also is an etiology—a story that explains why things are the way they are. It explains how groups of people came to be and why the Israelites are similar with yet different from their neighbors. The story tells too, why there are strange geological formations that seem to resemble human figures in the Dead Sea region: Lot's wife was turned into a pillar of salt. Similar stories are told in Hawai'i to explain distinctive land markings. When Kamapua'a tried to rape Pele, Pele's sister took her vagina and flung it to Hawai'i Kai to distract the pig man. The flying vagina landed with such impact that it made an impression on the terrain: Koko Crater.

There's a lot in the story of Lot and his family. The tale can be appreciated for its coarse humor and its attempt to make sense out of the non-sense. The story loses its appeal, however, when it is taken out of its context and forced into a contemporary tirade against homosexuality, as some have tried to do. According to the prophet Ezekiel, the wickedness of Sodom and Gomorrah was not homosexuality between consenting adults; but the blatant inhospitality towards visitors. Instead of welcoming visitors and caring for the needs of the stranger as required in the Bible, the people of Sodom threatened the visitors with sexual violence. Had Lot's guests been female instead, but subjected to the same threats of sexual assault, the city would have still been destroyed for its wickedness. If only one of Lot's guests had distracted his attackers by tossing his penis to a far away land instead—perhaps 'Iao Valley in Maui—the whole situation could have been avoided. But then again, we'd have different visitors to 'Iao Needle and the poor angel wouldn't be able to count to eleven.

Suicide In The Bible

Many of the issues that are pressing to us today were simply not considered important to people during the time of Jesus. Genetic engineering, LGBTQ rights and global warming, for example, were not concerns Jesus and his contemporaries knew anything about. The same goes for physician-assisted suicide. There is nothing in the Bible regarding physician-assisted suicide. Therefore, those who wish to use the Bible to support a position either for or against this end-of-life issue are faced with a challenge: how do you make the Bible say something it doesn't say?

This is a central question students in my Bible classes must consider. As part of their research assignment, I have students examine the ways in which a particular church uses the Bible to support its position on a selected ethical issue in contemporary society. Simply put, how does a church take a biblical position on an ethical issue when the Bible does not specifically address that issue?

While there are themes in the Bible that are powerful and beautiful (and disturbing) and timeless, there are also ethical and moral issues of vital concern only to people living in a particular place and in a particular time. We no longer live in those places and in those times. It is therefore difficult to apply the ideals of an ancient scriptural text to contemporary issues, as in many instances our values and beliefs have changed. For example, the Bible condemns divorce, but condones slavery; whereas our society does just the opposite. Those who look to the Bible for ethical guidance, therefore, must distinguish between values that are timeless and beliefs that are time-bound.

Many people assume the Bible condemns suicide. Students, however, are surprised to learn that the Bible does not explicitly condemn or prohibit taking one's own life. There are seven clear examples of suicide in the Bible—Abimelech, who asked for assistance to commit suicide because he was mortally wounded by a woman and didn't want it to be known that a woman had killed him; Samson, who asked God to let him die with his enemies (God obliged) by bringing down a house to crush himself and everyone in it; Saul, who fell on his own sword to avoid being killed by his enemies; Ahithophel, who hung himself after betraying King David; Zimri, who burned down his house after military defeat; and Judas, Jesus' disciple who hung himself after bringing the Roman authorities to arrest Jesus. There is nothing in any of the above stories that indicate the Bible writers disapproved of the suicides. Instead the stories uphold the noble-death ideal valued in ancient times (and in certain cultures today).

In antiquity, suicide was deemed a noble act if carried out to avoid capture on the battlefield, for the sake of one's country or loved ones, or in the face of intolerable pain, incurable disease, devastating misfortune or shame. The suicides in the Bible reflect this ethos. As such, the Bible does not condemn the suicides. If anything, the Bible writers convey a positive attitude to taking one's own life in two of the stories.

The suicide of Judas, for example, is portrayed as an act of atonement, carried out as a result of repentance. And God gave Samson strength to carry out the mass murder of his enemies. The biblical writer thus commends Samson's suicide because "those he killed at his death were more than those he had killed during his life." (Judges 16:30) Samson is the biblical equivalent of a suicide-bomber.

Suicide became viewed as a sin several hundred years after the death of Jesus, when Saint Augustine condemned his Christian opponents' vigorous embrace of a martyrdom ethic. Early Christians (and Jesus himself?) practiced martyrdom—which views self-death as a form of heroic witness. Martyrdom was seen as an act of discipleship and as a way to imitate Christ. However, as a means to delegitimize his opponents, Augustine denounced their practice of martyrdom as suicide and labeled suicide a sin. From this, those who committed suicide would be (and sadly still are in some places) denied a Christian burial. If it weren't for Augustine it is questionable whether suicide would be considered a sin by many Christian churches.

Because the Bible writers were not concerned with many of the ethical dilemmas that confront us today, all scriptural reading on the various issues is interpretation. Therefore, whenever someone quotes a biblical passage either in support of or against physician-assisted suicide, the person is revealing more about what is in his/her heart rather than what is in the Bible. The Bible simply doesn't have anything to say on the matter.

God's Name

Jews, Christians, and Muslims are religious siblings who claim to believe in the same God, but do they really? The Quran makes it clear that Allah is God in Islam, but what about the biblical God? What is

God's name there? Nobody knows. There are several reasons why no one can state with absolute certainty what the name of the biblical God is. Here are two:

There were no vowels written in ancient Hebrew. As a result, though it appears more than 6,800 times in the Bible, there was no clear pronunciation guide for God's four-letter name: YHWH (or YHVH). Most scholars think the sacred name may have been pronounced similar to Yahweh—for example the truncated version of the name ("Yah") appears in "hallelujah"—but again, no one can say for sure.

A second reason for not knowing the exact pronunciation of the biblical God's name can be traced to blasphemy laws. Misusing God's name was punishable by death as it violated notions of what was deemed sacred. The term "sacred" is Latin-derived and means, "to set apart." God is above and beyond everything else. God is therefore one—not simply in terms of quantity, but in quality as well. In short, nothing compares to God. This explains the prohibition of images of God in Judaism and Islam, for how can the infinite (God) be contained in the finite (clay, paint, wood, stone, etc.)? How can what is created hold the Creator? The Creator is set apart from creation. To violate the line of separation between God and creation is to commit blasphemy. Hence addressing God by his personal name violates this line. This explains why Jesus never addressed God by his personal name. Jesus was a Jew. He substituted a title—Abba (Father)—instead. The practice of substituting a title for a personal name is familiar to us. We don't address our parents or heads of state by their personal names, but with titles. Most would address our president with the title "Mr. President," and not by his personal name. The same principle applies to God, for if we use a title of respect to address a human being, how much more so should we use a reverential one to address the Supreme Being? What title was used for God?

Since it was considered blasphemy to pronounce YHWH, a substitute title was used. Adonai (vowels were added later to Hebrew), meaning "LORD," was written in the margins of the text to indicate this word was to be substituted for YHWH whenever the personal name of God appeared in the Bible. Jesus was a Jew, who attracted followers who were Jews, and they prayed to the God of the Jews, and observed the teachings and practices of the Jews, including the practice of not pronouncing God's personal name. Centuries later, however, the majority of Jesus' followers were no longer Jews, which meant they no longer observed Jewish practices. They did not keep the Sabbath holy (Saturday is the seventh day of the week; not Sunday), nor did they keep God's name sacred. Today, some Christians are quite happy to say God's personal name out loud, even when it's wrong.

Because no one knew how to pronounce YHWH, and because "adonai" was clearly associated with God's name, Christians took the vowels from "adonai" and inserted them into God's personal name. YHWH thus became Yahowah or Yahovah, which later became Jehovah. Jehovah is a mistranslation of God's sacred name. It is a misuse of the sacred name and violates one of the 10 Commandments. This may explain why some prayers go unanswered.

What is more, when Christians proclaim, "Jesus is LORD," they are asserting that Jesus is "adonai," meaning Jesus is God. For Jews and Muslims this is unacceptable. God the Creator is separate from the created. The declaration "Jesus is LORD," violates the sacred line of demarcation: it claims that the Created IS the Creator. For these reasons (and others) Jews and Muslims reject the belief that Jesus is God. For Christians, of course, this belief is central to their faith.

Names have the power to establish identity and regulate relationships. Names can also unite or divide. When it comes to the three religious siblings, it is clear which of the two occurs in the name of God.

Mrs. God

It's tough being a single parent. Just ask God. With more than 2 billion people ingratiating themselves to a heavenly father and beseeching him for favors, it's difficult to stay on top of things. People, places, and prayers don't always get the attention they deserve as a result.

If god is father, what happened to mom? Did the god of the Bible ever have a wife? Probably.

Asherah was a mother goddess of fertility and wife to the god El. El in turn was the chief deity of a collection of gods worshipped in Canaan, the region in which the Israelite religion developed. El ruled the cosmos and delegated responsibilities to the other gods, including the biblical god YHWH (Deuteronomy 32:8-9). El was called the "Father of Years" and the "Ancient of Days" and to express this, the Canaanites portrayed El with white hair and a long beard. That the Israelites incorporated belief in the god El into their religious practice is evident in the name *Israel*—which includes the name *El*—and several biblical passages that refer to God as the head of a divine council (1 Kings 22:19-22, Psalm 82:7 and Psalm 89:6-7). Of course a popular image of god depicts him as an old man with a long white beard. Originally separate deities, the Canaanite god El was later identified with the Israelite god YHWH. Was Asherah's association with El also transferred to the Israelite god?

A 1975 archaeological excavation of an Israelite religious site in the northern Sinai peninsula revealed large ceramic jars with the inscription "Yahweh and his Asherah." Interestingly, the inscription is accompanied by two bovine figures, which led some scholars to speculate that the golden calf in the story of Moses may have actually represented the Israelite god. (This explains the presence of horns in the sanctuary at the altar of god [1 Kings 2:28] and why golden calves were created as symbols of the god that led the Israelites out of Egypt [1 Kings 12:28].)

In portraits of Asherah, a tree is carved above her pubic area, signifying that as a fertility goddess, she is the tree of life. A tree, pillar, pole or grove thus came to symbolize Asherah. Asherah and her symbols appear about 50 times in the Bible, an indication of her prominence. If Asherah was god's wife, one would expect to find her in god's temple, worshipped alongside her husband. Indeed, this seems to have been the case (2 Kings 21:7, 2 Kings 23:6-7). A tree of life was also in the Garden of Eden. When the worship of Asherah fell out of favor after the destruction of Jerusalem in 587 BCE, biblical writers denounced her and tried to edit her out of popular worship. This accounts for the negative views about her in the

Bible. Yet it cannot be denied that the fact she is mentioned numerous times in the Bible tells us her appeal was widespread (1 Kings 14:23). As a matter of fact, archaeologists have unearthed an abundance of clay female figurines in ancient Israel dating from the eighth through the sixth centuries BCE. Numbering in the hundreds and found at both religious shrines and domestic sites, these figurines suggest that the female principle was an integral part of religious worship in pre-exilic Israel.

Women resisted the attempt to destroy worship of the goddess, even when a prophet of God demanded that they do so (Jeremiah 44:15-18). The women were defiant and vowed to continue to worship the "queen of heaven" (Jeremiah 7:17-18) because she blessed them with prosperity. If Asherah was God's wife, she offered women a sympathetic and maternal deity to whom they could turn. Without her, women were denied a voice in the official religion of Israel.

The attack and removal of the female divine principle in later biblical times have played an unfortunate role in the negative perception of women many have in our own time. I am surprised (and saddened) to regularly hear from some of the young women in my Bible classes that they do not believe women should hold primary leadership positions at places of worship, but be given only supporting roles in the ministry instead. Yet these same women get angry at sexist attitudes in the workplace or when their gender denies them the same opportunities in society as their male counterparts. There is a disconnect between their personal faith and their regular life. Why? The Bible editors who denounced and removed the veneration and celebration of the female principle from their religion have done a near thorough job. As a result, they've made God a single parent and have relegated women to inferior spiritual status in their own faith.

Satan

Poor Satan. He gets blamed for everything. He wasn't present in the Garden of Eden (read Genesis 3 and see for yourself), yet he is wrongly accused of tempting Adam and Eve and causing the downfall of humanity as a result. There should be a commandment against bearing false witness.

But Satan wasn't always bad, at least not according to the Bible. In fact, at one point Satan and God were on the same side. It was humans who were on the other. Complicating matters further, Satan didn't always exist, which explains why he cannot be found in the earliest books of the Bible. Where then did evil come from if not from Satan? God. God was the source of both good and evil in the early period of theological development expressed in the Bible.

In the view of religion scholars, the figure of Satan probably evolved in stages, originating from the negative qualities once attributed to God. From this perspective, in the earliest stage in the development of the Satan concept, God was viewed as the only divine principle in the universe thus God was the cause of everything—good and evil, joy and sorrow, prosperity and suffering, blessings and curses. This is plainly stated in Deuteronomy 28, Amos 4, and Isaiah 45:7, for example.

In a subsequent stage in the development of Satan, the dark, violent and destructive qualities of God begin to be separated from the deity. Here God dispatches an "evil spirit" (1 Samuel 16) or a "lying spirit" (1 Kings 22) to torment those who have fallen out of God's favor. God uses evil as a tool to impose his will. Remnants of this stage of development is also found in Ezekiel 20:25-26, where God boasts that he intentionally gave his people laws that were not good and practices that would horrify them to prove his might.

In a later development, God presided over a heavenly assembly and judged other gods based on the extent to which they fulfilled their responsibilities (Psalms 82). Satan's earliest appearance as a separate entity came in the role as a regular member of God's divine council. In the book of Job,

Satan is included among the "sons of God." In this period of development in the concept of Satan, Satan's job is to carry out God's orders. Satan is a servant of God who is tasked with "accusing" us and tests our loyalty to God. This is made clear in the books of Job and Zechariah, where Satan functions as a heavenly prosecuting attorney, presenting a case against the faith of humanity to God the judge. Sometimes God accepts Satan's argument (Job); sometimes he doesn't (Zechariah). However it should be kept in mind that during this stage of development, Satan is the adversary of humanity, not God. Satan is not independent from God and can do nothing without God's permission.

Satan emerges as an independent figure after the destruction of Jerusalem in 587 BCE, when Jews were forced into exile and live under the control of foreign powers. Foreign beliefs and ideas—including Persian and Greek notions of evil—begin to influence and shape the biblical religion. Satan is recast as God's opponent, a dark wicked force waging a cosmic battle against the righteous.

Perhaps the best example to illustrate the historical development of the Satan concept can be seen by looking at the views presented by two different books in the Bible (2 Samuel and 1 Chronicles) written hundreds of years apart (one before the Babylonian exile and one after) that describe the same event: the census by King David and the death of 70,000 men. People hated censuses because they were used for taxation purposes and for military conscription. In 2 Samuel 24, God causes David to take a census of the people and then punishes him for doing it by sending a plague that kills 70,000 men. This may seem odd (why would God cause David to do something terrible and then punish him for obeying his orders?), but at this stage there is no Satan figure yet. God is the source of all things. By the time 1 Chronicles was written, however, the concept of Satan had emerged and had been incorporated into the Bible. Thus in the 1 Chronicles 21 account, it is now Satan who is responsible for causing David to take the census of the people. God only punishes David for the act by killing 70,000 people. Who, then, caused David to take the fatal census—God or Satan? It depends on which biblical book you read.

By the time the last book that closes the Christian Bible was written, earlier biblical stories were reinterpreted to cast Satan as the devil (Revelation 12). Satan had now become a completely independent entity who opposes God, the supernatural embodiment of evil and the powerful master over an underworld of fire and brimstone. The concept of Satan as a religion professor and columnist would be developed later.

Same Books; Different Ideas

In matters of faith, the same set of writings can have two different interpretations, leading to two separate religions. This is the case with the Hebrew Bible (Judaism) and the Old Testament (Christianity).

On the one hand, the Hebrew Bible and the Old Testament are the same. They contain the same set of books, written by the same set of authors, and speak about the same God.

On the other hand, the Hebrew Bible and the Old Testament refer to very different texts. They were written in different languages, arranged in different ways, and reflect different beliefs.

The Hebrew Bible was originally written in Hebrew (obviously). The Hebrews were an ancient people and not many people know this, but the Hebrews invented coffee. The men had the task of making the coffee. That's why they were called, "He-Brews."

Kidding aside, the language of the Bible affects the content of the Bible. Two examples suffice here, one minor and one major. The Old Testament was based on the Greek translation of the Hebrew Bible. According to the Old Testament, God—through Moses—led his people out of bondage from Egypt and parted the Red Sea to do so. In the Hebrew Bible, however, God does not part the Red Sea, but the Sea of Reeds instead. Parting the Sea of Reeds continues a theme established in the first book of the Bible with the story of Noah, who was saved from death by drowning by entering an ark (Hebrew = *teva*) made from various materials, including gopher wood, which may have been a type of reed. Moses is also saved from death by being placed in a *teva* on the riverbank among the reeds. God will then save his people from drowning by leading them through the Sea of Reeds. This theme that connects the stories of Noah's ark, baby Moses, and the exodus from Egypt is broken by the Old Testament Red Sea translation.

There is no virgin birth in the Hebrew Bible. But there is one in the Old Testament, in the book of Isaiah (7:14): "Behold, a *virgin* is with child and shall bear a son, and shall name him Immanuel." The Hebrew Bible also has the book of Isaiah, but there it reads: "Behold, the *young woman* (almah) is with child and shall bear a son, and shall name him Immanuel." In Hebrew, *almah* refers simply to a young woman, regardless of her sexual status. The specific Hebrew word for virgin is *betula*, which is not used in Isaiah. In fact, not only does the Hebrew word *almah* NOT specify a virgin; *almah* can refer to an adulterous woman. (Proverbs 30:20) A virgin is slightly different from an adulterous woman. Nonetheless, when the Hebrew Bible was translated into Greek, *almah* became *parthenos,* the Greek word for virgin. This was significant for the development of Christianity, as the first book of the New Testament, Matthew, tells the story of the virgin birth of Jesus and states this fulfilled the prophecy of Isaiah. Except it doesn't in the Hebrew Bible, because there is no virgin birth prophecy in Isaiah.

Another way the Hebrew Bible and Old Testament differ is in the order that the books are arranged. The books of the Hebrew Bible are divided into three categories—Torah (laws), neviim (prophets) and kethuvim (writings)—with the last book, Chronicles, closing the Hebrew Bible. Chronicles ends by directing God's people to go to Jerusalem and the temple that will be rebuilt there. Thus for Jews, the Hebrew Bible points to Jerusalem and the temple, the most sacred site in all of Judaism.

The Old Testament, however, arranges its books in a different order. Chronicles is placed near the middle of the Old Testament. The last position in the Old Testament is reserved for the book of Malachi instead.

In the Hebrew Bible, Malachi is one of the minor prophets and is not a separate book, but is lumped together with eleven other minor prophets into one large book. What is the significance of Malachi for Christians? Malachi speaks of the coming Day of the Lord, and Christians believe the messianic promise of Malachi is fulfilled in Jesus Christ. Thus for Christians, the Old Testament points to the coming of Jesus Christ—the most sacred event in Christianity.

The Hebrew Bible and the Old Testament both emphasize the laws of God and the covenant with God. In fact, our English word *Testament* comes from the Latin word, *Testamentum,* which is based on the Greek word *diatheke,* itself the translation of the Hebrew word *Berit,* which is usually rendered as *covenant.* God establishes an eternal covenant with his people in the first book of the Bible (Genesis 17:7).

Interestingly, Christians believe the Old Testament is for them, yet they refuse to follow it. The Sabbath need not be observed, circumcision need not be practiced, dietary regulations don't have to be kept, images of God can be made, etc. This is part of the reason why it has the word *Old* in its title—the everlasting covenant was for a former time.

For Christians, God's covenant has been fulfilled and superseded by Jesus Christ, who has established a new covenant, a New Testament. For Jews, God's covenant cannot be replaced. It is not old or no longer valid. God's covenant is everlasting—at least it is in their Bible.

How Books Got Into the New Testament

My memory is bad. I know there are 26 letters in the alphabet, but when I try to recite them I only count 25. I don't know why (y). Most Christians know that there are 27 books in the New

Testament and many can recite all 27. But most do not know why these books were chosen to be in the Bible.

Christians wrote more than 27 books about Jesus and what it means to be a follower of Christ. For example, although there are only four gospels in the New Testament—Matthew, Mark, Luke, and John—many others were produced. There is the Gospel of Thomas, the Gospel of Mary, and the Gospel of Philip just to name a few. How then did the Christian Church decide on which 27 books to include in their Bible? Church leaders seemed to have employed four criteria that they considered especially important in determining the books of the New Testament: antiquity, apostolicity, confirmation, and consensus.

The 27 books in the New Testament were written between the years 50 and 150 CE. In other words, the earlier a book was written the higher the chance a book had for consideration in the Christian Bible. This is the criterion of *antiquity*. The earliest New Testament book is 1 Thessalonians, written around the year 50. The latest New Testament book is 2 Peter, produced around the year 150. As a point of reference, Jesus lived roughly between the years 3 BCE and 30 CE. In the view of scholars, Jesus did not write anything (or at least anything that we know of); nor did his disciples. There were two probable reasons for this: 1) not many people in antiquity knew how to write, 2) they expected the world to end soon (some Christians still do). As Jesus and his disciples died and the world did not come to an end, there arose a need for Christians to collect writings to preserve and communicate their faith. The church leaders therefore placed special importance on books written as close as possible to the time of Jesus.

The criterion of *apostolicity* emphasizes the source of the biblical book. A book had a higher chance of being included in the New Testament if a book was somehow associated with an apostle of Jesus. Again, because Jesus did not write anything, writings that may have been produced by his apostles were valued. This explains why Paul's writings were readily accepted as scripture, but Clement's letters were not (Clement was a bishop of Rome). To complicate things slightly, all the gospels in the New Testament were originally anonymous, but were later attributed to Jesus' apostles and associates—Matthew, Mark, Luke, John—to heighten their religious viability.

The criterion of *confirmation* focuses on the beliefs and ideas conveyed in the books themselves. Writings that advocated or confirmed the teachings of the developing Christian church had a higher chance of inclusion in the New Testament than writings that did not. For example, the Gospel of Thomas contains 114 sayings of Jesus and meets the criteria of antiquity and apostolicity. Yet Thomas was not accepted into the New Testament. Why not? Thomas does not mention the crucifixion or resurrection of Jesus, but states that salvation comes from a deep understanding of the secret words of Jesus instead. Moreover, the author claims to be Didymus Thomas—Jesus' twin! (Didymus is Greek for twin; Thomas is Aramaic for twin.) Here's another example: According to the Gospel of Mary and the Gospel of Philip, Jesus' closest disciple was Mary Magdalene, who was also his lover. The Gospel of Mary and the Gospel of Philip did not make it into the New Testament.

Consensus is the fourth criterion church leaders used to determine which books would be included in the New Testament. Simply put, a book had a higher chance for inclusion in the Christian Bible if it was used by a large number of churches, but especially if prominent churches used or favored the writing. The churches in Rome, Alexandria, and Antioch were particularly influential in this regard.

In the year 367 (337 years after the death of Jesus), Athanasius—bishop of Alexandria—wrote a letter to the various churches listing for the first time the 27 books of the New Testament that we have today. Athanasius specified that only these 27 books be accepted for inclusion into the New Testament. The various churches debated Athanasius' list of 27 books and it took several decades before most Christian churches agreed upon the books that make up the New Testament. Some of my Christian friends told me that the 27 books came about simply as a result of much praying. But *praying* is based on the Old French word *preier*. I guess they also didn't know why (y).

ON BUDDHISM

Anatman

My bathroom scale doesn't work. It is 11 pounds off. I know this because the weight I see when I step on the scale does not match the image I have of myself. In fact, my bathroom mirror is defective too. When I look into it, I see someone I don't recognize. I see a person getting old and falling out of shape. My wife tries to console me. She tells me that I'm still in shape because oval is a shape.

Sometimes I long for my younger days. I know I'm good looking now, but you should have seen me when I was in my 20s. I was so good-looking—I think I was illegal. That person has since surrendered to the laws of aging and time.

Time is measured in different ways in Buddhism, broken into big units (kalpa) and small units (ksana). The longest kalpa lasts for an incalculable eon while numerous ksanas pass within a single instant. Furthermore, within each ksana countless sets of arising and ceasing of phenomena take place. There are thus continuous changes occurring at each moment, even if we don't perceive them. We change because change is the essence of time and time is the substance we are made of.

There is an amusingly grotesque Buddhist story that tells of a man traveling alone in the woods who became lost. It got late and it began to rain, so the man sought shelter in an abandoned hut to wait out the rain. Since it was late and he was tired, he soon fell asleep. Suddenly he heard loud noises and awoke to find that he was not in an abandoned hut as he had thought, but in the hut of a demon that had dragged in a corpse. A second demon soon entered the hut and claimed the corpse for itself. They began to argue over which demon owned the body when they saw the man cowering in the corner. They decided to ask the trembling man to decide the matter and tell them to whom the body belonged. He of course didn't know. Worse still, he knew that whichever demon he chose the other would be upset and harm him. Seeing that there was no escape from the situation and that his tormentors demanded that he choose between the two demons, he said, "Uh,…I choose my mother-in-law." (I'm joking—he chose the other menacing figure.) Just as he feared, the angry demon tore off his arm and tossed it to the ground. The other demon ripped an arm off the corpse and replaced the lost arm. The angry demon then tore off the man's other arm and hurled it outside the hut, but the other demon ripped off the other arm from the corpse and plugged it into the man. This infuriated the angry demon even more, so he ate off one of the man's legs. But the other demon, now thoroughly delighted, replaced it with the leg of the corpse. This went on until every body part of the unfortunate man was torn away and replaced by the limbs from the corpse. When the two demons realized what they had done, they had a good laugh, picked up some of the body parts scattered on the ground and devoured them. They then went out of the hut, leaving the poor man to ponder the question who was he? Did he consist of body parts scattered on the ground and in the belly of demons, or was he made up of the limbs of a corpse?

This story is told to illustrate the Buddhist concept of anatman— non-permanent self. We are born, we grow up, we grow old, we die. Sometimes we grow apart. And as the story graphically describes: we also can fall apart. We are constantly changing, in subtle and not so subtle ways. To cling to a set image of oneself is to invite dukkha—unsatisfactoriness, disappointment, and suffering.

Since we change, it is natural that our relationships do too. My wife and I have been married for 20 years. My wife will tell you that sometimes the years feel like ksana; sometimes they feel like kalpa. Those of us in long-term relationships know that the most dangerous threat to a lasting relationship is the tendency to take the other person for granted. We fall into routines and mistakenly think nothing changes. This is illusion. The reality is everything is in constant change and nothing lasts. 20 summers ago, I married a beautiful young woman in a church in Scotland. That woman is gone. Now, when I wake up in the morning and I look over to my side, that young beautiful woman I married has been replaced by someone…even more beautiful.

All of our relationships will come to an end, either because of separation or death. This is an unsettling thought, especially when we think about our loved ones. And yet, Buddhism has an optimistic approach to this fate.

Buddhism teaches that each moment is all that there is and will never occur again. Each moment therefore is precious. Understanding this deepens our appreciation for our experiences, relationships, and time.

Eternal life doesn't appeal to me. It is the knowledge that I'm going to die that makes me live. It brings a joy to being alive and creates the need to let my loved ones know how much they mean to me while I am alive and while they are still here. If we live forever, why bother to say or do anything because there will always be tomorrow? My tomorrows are limited. And should I ever forget this, my bathroom scale and mirror will remind me.

Buddhism & Suffering

Buddhism isn't about how you look. It's more about how you see. In fact the word "Buddha" is related to the word "see." Not so much "see" in the physical sense, but more akin to "see" as in spiritual understanding. For example, when we finally understand something, we say we "see." Moreover, the word "religion" literally means, "connect again." Thus Buddhism helps one to see the world in a certain way, to see connections between what is sacred and what is ordinary, and to see the ways in which causes and conditions arise and impact our lives. In short, Buddhism helps one to see the connections between the individual and the world, how we are shapers of and shaped by the world around us and the world within us.

There are several themes that underpin the teachings in Buddhism, including the notion that life is conditioned by suffering and impermanence. Because of the focus on suffering and impermanence, some view Buddhism as a pessimistic religion. Buddhists, however, argue that their religion is not pessimistic, but realistic: impermanence is a fact of life. In the midst of joy there is already the loss of joy. Ultimately, however, Buddhists say that Buddhism is an optimistic religion if one sees things from a proper perspective. We all suffer, but in the midst of suffering there is already the end of suffering.

The problem of suffering, then, is not how to avoid suffering, but how to transform it. We may not be able to always control what happens to us, but we can exercise control over how we respond to what happens to us. And if one can control the mind, one can control one's self and—to a certain extent—one's world.

One of the most popular stories in Buddhism is about a young woman, Kisa Gotami, who woke up one morning to find her baby boy dead. She frantically ran to her neighbors' homes carrying her dead baby and pounded on the doors, begging people to help her. People thought she had lost her mind because her grief was so great. One neighbor told her to go see the Buddha, who was nearby. Kisa Gotami rushed to the Buddha still carrying her dead baby and pleaded with the Buddha to give her medicine that would help her. The Buddha told her to get a handful of mustard seeds, one seed from each family where no one had died. She desperately went from home to home, but she could not find a house that had not suffered the death of a family member. Instead, she heard stories of others who had lost loved ones too. With each house Kisa Gotami began to see and understand that death is a part of life. Moreover, as she shared her story of her son's death with others and they their stories of heartache with her, her suffering began to be transformed. Grief shared is grief lessened. There is a word intimately connected to suffering—compassion—that literally means to "suffer with." The sorrow she had for herself at the start transformed into compassion she felt for others in the end. She gave her son a proper funeral and was thankful for the precious time, as short as it was, that he was a part of her life. She then returned to the Buddha, who comforted her and she became a follower.

Some may wonder why the Buddha did not resurrect the dead baby? In other religions this sort of miracle would have been expected, why not here? If the Buddha had brought the child back to life, his mother would undoubtedly have been happy. But what if the child died again, what would his mother do then? How many times would the Buddha have to restore the dead to life in order for one to be satisfied? Denying death does not alleviate suffering or bring happiness. It deepens grief when death occurs instead. On the other hand, accepting death and understanding that each moment is a link to all that came before and all that will follow and—most importantly—will never occur again, inspires us to live our lives fully. There is an eternity of connections in each moment and realizing this encourages us to create meaningful and truly happy lives. Instead of healing the body, the Buddha healed Kisa Gotami's mind and helped her to see and understand the meaning of life.

Religions are meaning producing systems that help us transform suffering into something bearable, manageable, and even meaningful. The Buddha's teaching on suffering connects us to each other and to the world around us. We all suffer. However, suffering can be transformed into compassion, and from this endurance, honor, the renewal of hope and meaning will follow. There is a world of possibility in each moment, if one takes the time to see.

A Buddhist Serial Killer

Fingers and hands help us to see and understand. They can clear our paths and point us in the right direction. But they can also cover our eyes and blind us. A Chinese proverb says, "When a finger points to the moon, the fool looks at the finger." Here's a well-known Buddhist tale about looking only at the fingers.

Angulimala was a serial killer who was saved by the Buddha's teachings. Angulimala was initially a practitioner of ahimsa (non-injury) and loving kindness, but due to a cruel twist of fate, he fell into a situation where he was tasked with procuring 1,000 fingers—one from a thousand different people—and had to kill in order to do so. Angulimala was traumatized after his first murder because he had violated his lifelong principles of non-violence and compassion. He had trouble slicing off the finger of his victim. With each killing, however, things got easier. Wrongful acts no longer bothered him as much. His mind became jaded and he became obsessed with fingers. With each finger obtained, he lost further touch with reality. Instead of taking fingers, the fingers began taking him. In other words, he became possessed by his possessions. The well-being of others no longer mattered, and when he looked at a person he did not see the whole person, he was only interested in the person's body parts. (Some of my college students are like this.) His obsession with fingers was such that he did not want to sleep for fear of losing any of his collected fingers. And when he finally slept, it was not restful, as he dreamt only of obtaining more fingers. His fixation with fingers became such that he strung the cutoff fingers together in a necklace and wore them around his neck. In fact, his name "Angulimala" means, "garland of fingers." After obtaining his 999th finger, he decided his last killing would be special. He would make his victim suffer a little longer so that he could enjoy taking the finger a little more. He hid in the forest waiting for his unsuspecting victim to appear, eagerly anticipating the look of terror that would spread across his victim's face at the sight of him. Who would be Angulimala's 1000th victim? His mother. Parents love unconditionally, and Angulimala's mother wanted to help her son. When Angulimala saw her, he was distraught. "Why, mother, did it have to be you? Oh well, too bad…" A deranged mind will even turn on family. Fortunately for the mother, the Buddha was nearby, and when he saw the woman entering the forest, he stepped in front of her and walked in first. "Thank you, Buddha, for saving my mother—but now I will get you." Angulimala jumped out from behind the tree and tried to stop the Buddha and attack him, but he couldn't. He could not grab hold of the Buddha, even though the Buddha simply walked. After cursing and shouting several times at the Buddha to stop, the Buddha turned to Angulimala and said, "I have stopped, Angulimala. I have stopped being attached to the values of the world. I have stopped chasing after desires and hurting others. It is you, Angulimala, who must stop." At these words it is said the illusion that had engulfed Angulimala all those years was shattered, the darkness that entrapped him for so long was destroyed. The Buddha helped Angulimala emerge from the darkness where he could not see, and into the light where he could. Fingers no longer clouded his vision. Angulimala began to "see" and he let go of the fingers.

Angulimala became a follower of the Buddha. As a wandering monk, his fingers and hands no longer took what was not his—they now carried a begging bowl to accept whatever was given to him. Angulimala was deeply moved when he came across a woman suffering a breech birth and bestowed a blessing upon her to help her and her unborn baby. The baby was born safely and the mother and child were well as a result. A life-taker was now a life-giver. Buddhists today recite Angulimala's blessing for expectant mothers. The story of Angulimala ends with people beating Angulimala for his earlier life as a murderer. Angulimala returned from a morning round of begging with his head broken open and bleeding, his begging bowl broken, and his robes ripped to shreds.

As each year passes, it is not always easy to know how much to cling to from the past and what to let go of for the future. New challenges await and it is sometimes difficult to discern the opportunities that should be embraced from the temptations best resisted. Relationships, possessions, self-identities, traditions and especially religions—they are Angulimala's fingers. They can possess and blind us. The story of Angulimala reminds us that fingers and hands can cling, grasp and hold. But they also can help us to let go and accept what is waiting for us.

The Soul In Buddhism

Buddhist souls are a confused lot. They are not certain where to go or if they should even exist. There are 3 Characteristics of Existence in Buddhism—non-self, impermanence, suffering—and according to the concept of anatman (non-self), souls do not possess an eternal substantive essence. It is an illusion to think otherwise. Based on the numerous memorial rites and practices of ancestor veneration at the local Buddhist temples to appease the dead, however, it is clear not many of the lingering spirits are aware of this.

From the Buddhist point of view, what is thought of as the soul or self is an amalgamation of physical and psychological components, a combination of ever-changing material and mental forces or energies (skandhas). When one component changes, the self is no longer the same self. Indeed, science tells us that the cells in our bodies are in a process of constant change and renewal, and as a result, every seven years or so our bodies are replaced with a different one. (See photographs of yourself 7 years ago for evidence of this.)

Intimately connected to the principle of non-self is the teaching of anicca (impermanence), which states that nothing has any real, lasting, permanent, inherent nature. Everything is transient. Even the most ardent religious practitioner will admit that one's faith does not remain the same. Those who fail to realize this characteristic of existence cling to ideas, things, people and gods, investing themselves in their attachments and chained to them in return. Frustration and misery are the by-products of clinging to things that don't last. This condition marks the third characteristic of existence—the reality of suffering (dukkha).

The Buddha taught that there are several kinds of suffering, the most profound of which is caused by failing to understand anatman and anicca and being attached to illusion as a consequence. Imaginary and false beliefs produce craving, selfish desire, and attachment. Where is the soul in all this? Does it grasp and cling to us or we to it?

When the Buddha was asked whether or not there was a self, whether or not there was existence before birth, and whether or not there is existence after death, the Buddha refused to answer. The questions are products of extreme views and engaging in such discussions results in, and is the result of attachment to the self.

The Buddha's refusal to respond may have unwittingly produced an incompatibility between the fundamental Buddhist concept of impermanence on the one hand, with discourses and practices stressing the continued existence of the spirits of the deceased on the other. Temples and priests try to manage this tension, upholding the teaching of non-permanent self all the while performing rites for an ever-present soul. Is there a contradiction here between the impermanent existence of the self and permanent non-existence of the soul? In Buddhist discussions regarding orthodoxy, one side of the equation is often cited and used as a standard of authenticity to judge the other side.

The result is an unclear understanding of what the spirit is and where it exists.

The rituals imply the souls are still here when the teachings say they should be someplace else; they just don't know where.

Are they in the Pure Land of eternal bliss of Amitabha Buddha or do they reside in local graves or in memorial tablets placed on temple and home altars? Have they reached the ultimate state of nirvana? Are they enlightened? Why, then, must they return every summer for Obon? Why must they go anywhere? Indeed, do their very presence contradict the Buddha's teachings?

The 3 Characteristics of Existence—non-self, impermanence, suffering—do not apply to beings that don't exist. The dead don't exist. Yet the non-existent can be real and powerful. Just ask any person of faith. In this way, the spirits of the deceased continue to be present among the living. Life may be impermanent, but death is not.

If, after all this, Buddhist spirits are still unclear about where to go and seek a more definitive answer, they might consider asking the followers of Allah or Christ. They are almost certain to receive an unambiguous response there.

The Buddha Of Popularity

The most popular Buddha in Buddhism is not the Buddha—or it is not the historical Buddha, to be exact. The most popular Buddha is Amitabha (Chn. Amituo Fo; Kor. Amita Bul; Jpn. Amida Butsu; Viet. Adida Phat), the buddha who dwells in the Pure Land in the west. A visit to many of the local Buddhist temples will bear witness to the popularity of this Buddha, as it is not uncommon to see Amitabha on the main altar of worship rather than Siddhartha Gautama, the historical founder of Buddhism. Non-Buddhists might find this rather odd. It would be similar to walking into a Christian church where someone other than Jesus is venerated as the main figure of worship.

Why is Amitabha so popular? One reason is Amitabha's ability to save all beings. According to an account in *The Sutra of the Buddha of Immeasurable Life,* before Amitabha became a Buddha he made 48 vows, promising that were he not to fulfill any one of them, he would abandon his quest for enlightenment. Of the 48 vows that highlight the various virtues of his Pure Land, the 18th is of particular importance. There, Amitabha links his own enlightenment with the salvation of others. In short, Amitabha vowed that he would not become a Buddha unless he could save all those who are sincere in heart and have the desire to be born in his Pure Land. Amitabha has since become a Buddha, which means he has fulfilled his vows, including his promise of salvation.

Amitabha is thus the compassionate Buddha of infinite light and infinite life. He can save those who simply call his name and entrust themselves to him. Observing strict precepts or performing complicated rituals thus bears little consequence on matters of salvation. Instead, it is common practice at temples to hear followers recite the name of Amitabha as part of their prayers.

Some believe the simple recitation of a set phrase that calls the name of Amitabha is a sufficient act for rebirth in his Pure Land. One only needs to recite this phrase (Chn. Namo Amituo Fo; Kor. Namu Amita Bul; Jpn. Namu Amida Butsu; Viet. Namu Adida Phat) as few as ten times in a lifetime to ensure entrance into Amitabha's Pure Land. Others believe faith in Amitabha's vows are enough for rebirth and recite his name as an expression of gratitude for his promised salvation.

Amitabha's 19th vow is also important. There he promises to appear to believers at death to welcome them into his Pure Land. From this arose a tradition of believers facing west on their deathbeds (the direction of Amitabha's Pure Land) and holding onto one end of a cord woven of five-colored threads while the other end is placed in the hand of Amitabha. At death Amitabha would lead the faithful to his western paradise.

In Buddhist cosmology, the Pure Land is not heaven. It is beyond heaven. Some mistakenly think heaven is the highest realm of existence, but this is not so in Buddhism. While those in heaven indeed experience profound states of bliss, they are also eventually susceptible to change and degeneration. Those in the Pure Land of Amitabha, however, are not. (Indeed, Satan discovered that heaven is not eternal as he was cast out of heaven in the Biblical and Quranic traditions.) Amitabha created his Pure Land by taking the essence of what was best of all the various Buddha-fields and heaven-like states and bringing them together into one Pure Land.

While there are other pure lands in Buddhism, the Pure Land of Amitabha is located in the west, which is why—for those familiar with the lantern floating ceremony during Obon—the Obon lanterns always float towards the west, in the direction of the Pure Land of Amitabha.

What is the relationship between Siddhartha Gautama—the historical Buddha—and Amitabha? At first glance there seems to be little. Siddhartha Gautama—through his teachings such as the Four Noble Truths and the Middle Way—emphasized the impermanence of all things (even the soul), non-attachment and the end of suffering through the negation of desires. Amitabha, by contrast, promises eternal life, the attainment of countless treasures and joy through the fulfillment of one's desires—including fancy clothes, riches, perfect bodies and great families. Which Buddha would you place on your altar?

Jizo

One of the most popular figures in Japanese Buddhism is the bodhisattva Jizo. Statues of Jizo can be seen at many of the local Buddhist temples—Zaoji in Kalihi, Jodo Mission in Makiki, Koganji in Mānoa, Palolo Kwannon Temple, Liliha Shingon Mission, Gedatsukai in Kuliouou, and Wahiawa Ryusenji Soto Mission, for example. He is often standing outside the temple, bald, holding a staff, and sporting a red bib. Charged with the task of saving people from all walks of life, Jizo provides protection and compassion in numerous and diverse ways. Stories abound of the wondrous powers of Jizo. Jizo comes in several forms, each specializing in a particular area of concern. There is the Jizo who relieves the pain of those suffering from various physical ailments (Togenuki Jizo), a Jizo who offers protection and guidance to children (Koyasu Jizo), and a Jizo who improves the looks of those of us not blessed with physical beauty (Oshiroi Jizo). In Hawai'i, Jizo statues were also placed near the seashore to protect swimmers and fishermen alike. Indeed, a Jizo statue still stands guard near the Blow Hole lookout in east O'ahu. There is even a Jizo who extends salvation to children who did not quite make it to this world, namely the spirits of aborted fetuses or of babies lost due to miscarriages and stillbirths (Mizuko Jizo).

In this regard Jizo has not only garnered praise for his compassion, but controversy as well. In recent decades a popular if controversial practice in Japanese Buddhism that has made its way to American Buddhism is the rite known as mizuko kuyo. Mizuko kuyo is also observed at some of the local temples here. Mizuko kuyo is a memorial ritual for children who have died young, but is especially associated with abortions, miscarriages, and stillbirths. While there are various and sometimes conflicting interpretations of the ritual, it is generally believed that mizuko kuyo provides help to the spirits of the unborn suffering in the spiritual world and comfort to its living relatives in this world. Towards this end family members offer prayers to Jizo and may dress his statue in baby clothes (mittens, cap, bib) or place stuffed animals and other toys in his arms to assist him in finding, and saving, the spirit of their lost child.

The ritual is conducted at mostly Buddhist temples and family members may observe the rite on a continued basis years after the loss of the child. Critics charge that mizuko kuyo is exploitative, exacting high prices for the ritual while playing on the fears and sorrows of those who have lost children. Certain mizuko kuyo advertisements in Japan, for example, imply that bad luck will follow parents and family members if the rite is not performed to pacify the anguishing spirits. Advocates, on the other hand, view mizuko kuyo as a way to come to terms with a traumatic event and helps parents and siblings maintain a meaningful relationship with a deceased family member. Indeed, this is the emphasis in mizuko kuyo observed in American Buddhism. While the popularity—and controversy—of mizuko kuyo has not reached the same level here as elsewhere, the rite can be performed for anyone requesting it at a number of temples on the island.

Of course employing gods and deities to address contemporary social issues and trends is not something unique to Japanese Buddhism. Students tell me that other religious groups on the island use surfing ministries, dance ministries, and singles' ministries to attract followers and promote their gods. Are surfing ministries and mizuko kuyo acts of saving compassion or simply exploitation? As is often the case with such issues, the line between the two is not clearly drawn. What is clear, however, is this: With Jesus saving surfers and Jizo saving aborted fetuses, Hawai'i is truly paradise for anguishing souls.

The Merciful Bodhisattva

There are roughly seven billion bodhisattvas in the world. Bodhisattvas are beings of enlightenment in Mahayana Buddhism (the Buddhist tradition prominent in countries such as China, Korea, Japan, Tibet, and Vietnam). How is a bodhisattva different from a Buddha? One difference between the two is this: while Buddhas mostly reside in other realms and offer salvation to followers by bringing them to their worlds, bodhisattvas dwell in this world and help followers with this-worldly issues. No challenge is too great or desire too trivial for the bodhisattva. If it is important to followers, it is important to the bodhisattva.

Perhaps the most popular bodhisattva of them all is Avalokiteshvara—the bodhisattva of compassion and mercy—though this enlightened being is not usually known by this name. Devotees know Avalokiteshvara better as Kuan Yin (Chinese), Kwan Seum (Korean) or Kannon (Japanese).

Avalokiteshvara appears in some of the most widely known sutras in Mahayana Buddhism, for example in the Heart Sutra and the Lotus Sutra. What is more, according to chapter 25 of the Lotus Sutra, Kuan Yin/Kwan Seum/Kannon may appear in different forms—33 in all—in order to address the sufferings and needs of believers and to lead them to enlightenment. One of the best known of the 33 forms is the multi-headed, 1,000-armed Kuan Yin/Kwan Seum/Kannon. In this form, Avalokiteshvara has several heads to see the sufferings of people and hear the cries of the world, and a thousand arms to help alleviate the pain. Images of Avalokiteshvara in this form are venerated at some of the local Buddhist temples, including Palolo Kwannon Temple, Tendai Mission of Hawai'i and Tan Wah Temple in Nu'uanu.

The belief that Kannon can help believers deal with pressing issues in contemporary society can be seen in the distinctive forms Kannon assumes in Japan that go beyond the traditional 33. Japan has one of the highest—if not the highest—life expectancy average of any country in the world. At first glance, living longer may seem like a good thing. However, with advanced age comes a host of other problems—including the heightened possibility of dementia and a financial burden placed on families to care for their aged loved ones. These concerns have led to the appearance of unique forms of the bodhisattva of compassion. For example, Boke Fuji (Anti-senility) Kannon—to whom followers can pray to prevent dementia; and Sudden Death temples—where the elderly can pray to Kannon to bless them with a quick and painless death—are innovations of the Avalokiteshvara tradition that affirm the power of Kannon to address contemporary concerns. Indeed, on a trip to one of these temples in Japan, I purchased a specially blessed Kannon pillow that purports to prevent memory loss. I don't remember where I put it.

Avalokiteshvara often accompanies Amitabha Buddha (the Buddha who dwells in the western Pure Land) in images and on temple altars. According to legend, Avalokiteshvara was created from a beam of light that radiated from the forehead of Amitabha, thus the two are closely connected. Originally viewed as a male Buddhist figure in India, Avalokiteshvara underwent a gender transformation as Buddhism made its way to other countries and is commonly depicted in female form in China, Korea, and Japan. Elsewhere Avalokiteshvara still maintains his male form, in Tibet for example. In fact, followers believe the world-famous Dalai Lama is an incarnation of Avalokiteshvara. In the Tibetan Buddhist tradition, the religious leader known as the Panchen Lama has the responsibility of identifying the next reincarnated Dalai Lama after the former one passes away. In turn, the Dalai Lama identifies the future Panchen Lama. Why the close relationship between the two? The Panchen Lama is believed to be the incarnation of Amitabha Buddha.

It can be said that the bodhisattva who looks upon the world with compassion has assumed yet another form to help people see and appreciate the world in all its different manifestations. One of the devotees of this bodhisattva was a man named Goro Yoshida (1900-1993), who was one of the founders of a camera company in Japan. He named his camera Kannon. What better name to give to a camera than the name of the enlightened being who sees the world in all its myriad forms? Though the name of this camera company has since been altered slightly, Canon cameras help photographers shed light on the world within us through the photos they capture of the world around us. In this way Avalokiteshvara continues to cultivate the bodhisattva potential that dwells in each of us.

A Hand In Mudras

Mudras are sacred hand gestures prominent in Buddhism and other religions. Just as we use hand gestures to express what's in our hearts and minds, the various Buddhas display mudras to tell us who they are and give us insight into the powers and teachings they convey. Buddhist followers too, routinely perform mudras in their worship practices to communicate spiritual truths.

Fingers and hands tell us what's inside. They also guard us from dangers that threaten us from the outside. This explains in part the presence of fierce-looking statues with weapons in their hands placed at the entrance to some Buddhist temples. They brandish weapons to chase away those with ill intentions.

Inside the temples the Buddhas offer different kinds of mudras. There is the mudra of welcoming and blessing (open left hand placed waist high pointing downward with palm facing outward), and a mudra to comfort us and tell us to "fear not" (open right hand placed chest high with palm facing outward and fingers extending upward). Another common mudra is the meditation mudra. Formed by placing both hands in the lap, one on top of the other with palms turned upward and thumbs touching to form a circle, the meditation mudra is often associated with the Buddha in a seated position. One hand symbolizes the world of enlightenment; the other hand illusion. This mudra thus asserts the triumph of enlightenment over the world of illusion, though the two are intimately connected, as expressed by the touching thumbs. Images of the Buddhas are often depicted with the eyes half-open and half-closed, symbolizing the ability of the Buddhas to watch over the outside world around us as well as to help us see and reflect on the world within us.

Some temples have a standing Buddha on the main altar displaying a mudra similar to the "welcome" and "no fear" mudra described above, but with the thumb and index finger on each hand touching to form a circle that symbolizes the wisdom and compassion of enlightenment in complete harmony. This Buddha leans slightly forward to indicate a readiness to save all beings. A less common mudra displayed by some of the Buddhas is formed with one finger pointed while the other fingers are closed in a fist. This is a threatening mudra and warns evil to stay away.

Gassho is perhaps the best-known Buddhist mudra. When Buddhists pray, they place their palms together in a symbol of the unity of opposites or complements: oneself and others, wisdom and ignorance, past and present, life and death, the Buddha and all beings. Prayer beads—representing the teachings of the Buddha—are often held around both hands during gassho. Through the embrace of the Buddha's teachings, followers see that opposites are really one. Gassho expresses the inter-connectedness we share with each other and the gratitude that arises from this realization.

The best-known local mudra, however, is the shaka sign. A student in one of my religion classes shared how a Buddhist minister offered an interesting interpretation of our distinctive local gesture. In Japanese, the thumb is called the "parent finger" (oya-yubi) and the pinky is the "child finger" (ko-yubi). When one makes the shaka sign, a universal truth is expressed: the parent looks at the child, but the child looks in a different direction. This is natural. We lovingly watch over our children, but raise them to be independent and find their own paths, so that they can one day succeed when we are no longer around. This is good. A famous Buddhist story illustrates this: When a rich man asked a Buddhist monk to confer a blessing on his family that would guarantee prosperity, the monk simply offered, "Grandfather dies; father dies; son dies." In response to the shock and anger of the rich man at being told this, the monk wondered whether the man would prefer his family to experience the events in a different order. For one's family to experience life in its natural sequence is true happiness. Flashing the shaka sign thus conveys this universal truth and communicates that things are good.

Fingers and hands grasp and cling or they can reject and push away. They can also embrace, appreciate, and let go. They express what's in our hearts and minds. Indeed, the hand is the visible part of the mind.

Our eyes are such that they only see outwardly. Mudras help one to see inwardly as well. They point to who we are. Mudras help us to see that we are connected to the past, to the future, to each other, and to the world around us. They are outward physical signs of inward spiritual states. The next time you see an image of the Buddha, therefore, look closely at the hands. The Buddha may be offering you a hand; or the Buddha may simply be giving you the finger.

Cremation

It takes about two hours to cremate a body. Of course this is dependent on the size of the body (a child's body usually takes only an hour) and the level of heat used. At most crematoriums, the cremation chamber temperature is set between 1400 to 1600 degrees Fahrenheit. Many of my students were unaware of this when I asked the class to guess the degree of heat necessary to properly cremate a body. One student blurted out, "400 degrees!" Good guess, but the crematoriums are not baking brownies. Another student asked, "Why not set the temperature to 5000 degrees and be over with it?" There are two reasons why this isn't done: Too high heat and the arms of the deceased will rise in the chamber or the body may curl upward like a fish on a grill. Such a sight would disturb family members. More importantly, cremation at such high heat and the bones crumble into ashes. What's wrong with this?

In a number of cultures influenced by Buddhism, part of the funeral customs involves the collection of bone fragments of the cremated deceased. In Japan, this bone-picking ritual is called "kotsuage." After the body is cremated, family members pick up the bone fragments with mismatched chopsticks and pass them to each other before placing the bone fragments in an urn (feet first so that the deceased will not be stored upside down). The mismatched chopsticks symbolize the separation between the world of the living and the dead. The last piece of bone placed in the urn is the "nodo-botoke," or Adam's apple, because it resembles the shape of a Buddha sitting in meditation. This bone is carefully packed into the top of the urn, just under a piece of skull. In order to perform this ceremony then, care must be taken to cremate the body at the right temperature. Too low heat and the bones will be left too large to fit in the urn. Too high and only ashes will remain. Because of traditions surrounding this bone-picking ritual, it is considered a breach of social etiquette to pass food directly from chopstick to chopstick, or to use mismatched chopsticks.

Though death rituals and their meanings vary greatly in Buddhist cultures, cremation is commonly practiced as a means to free the spirit of the deceased from attachment to this world and facilitate its journey to the next. The characteristic chanting by Buddhist priests at funerals, often unintelligible to listeners, is meant to ready the spirit of the deceased for the other world. The spirit of the deceased is transformed through symbolic ordination, sutra chanting, and other rites designed to help the dead attain repose or enlightenment. In some ways, the Buddhist funeral is only the start of a journey that helps the spirit of the deceased transition from immediate family member to the realm of the ancestors. A series of memorial rites follow days, weeks, and even years after the cremation and funeral to assist in this transition. One of the most important of these rites is the 49th day memorial service. A common belief in many forms of Buddhism is the notion that it takes 49 days for the spirit of the deceased to leave this world and journey to the next. The 49th day memorial service completes the transformation of the dead from a spirit that is prayed for to an ancestor that is prayed to. (In many cultures and religions the number 7 symbolizes completion/perfection. 49 is simply seven times seven.) In some cultures a new spiritual name is given to the deceased as a symbol of this change in status. The new name may be written on a memorial tablet and kept at the home altar or placed in the temple, where offerings and prayers are dedicated to the deceased.

Cremation and the accompanying death rituals keep the dead alive. By creating and regulating relationships between the living and the dead, death rituals and memorial rites keep the spirit of the deceased apart from the world of the living and yet a part of the lives of the living. People may die, but relationships go on. The rites communicate meanings and memories of loved ones, allowing our relationships with the deceased to continue. And as long as the dead still have a presence in our lives, death does not kill completely.

Buddhist Halloween

Preta are not pretty. No one would want to take a selfie standing next to these grotesque figures. Preta have swollen bellies, deformed mouths, and throats as thin as a needle. If you find them wandering to your door on Halloween, be warned: no amount of candy will satisfy these mournful beings and no treats of any kind will relieve them of their sorrows.

Preta are miserable spirits of the deceased in the religious traditions of India (Hinduism, Buddhism, Jainism). However, as Buddhism traveled to China and Japan and interacted with the religious traditions there, preta also became known as "hungry ghosts." How did they become hungry in China and Japan? Ghosts don't like to reveal what they eat, but Chinese and Japanese like shoyu.

Actually, they were reborn as hungry ghosts because of two reasons: due to the neglect of others and due to their own moral failings.

Some believe those in this world who neglect the spirits of those who dwell in the other world create hungry ghosts. Because the living have forgotten their obligation to remember the dead and care for their spirit by observing proper death rituals and memorial rites, the spirits of the deceased become hungry ghosts that roam the spirit world looking for food and attention. They sometimes cross over into our world when doing so. The good news is that preta can be saved through the actions of their still living relatives. Special religious services can be conducted that make offerings to appease these wandering spirits.

Others think preta are created by the way one lives. In the Buddhist tradition, those who lead lives of unrestrained desire or jealousy or selfishness are reborn as preta.

Their appearance as ghastly figures is a metaphor for their spiritual state. Their gigantic bellies symbolize the relentless craving and enormous appetites they had while alive and still are enslaved to. Their slender necks signify their very limited ability to satisfy those appetites or soothe their constant cravings. Their poor moral traits have taken shape in the form of preta. These miserable beings utter mournful sounds to bemoan their unfortunate spiritual state. People who are never satisfied with what they have or who are constantly envious of others are in danger of being reborn as preta.

Left unchecked, preta may wander in their search for comfort and cause mischief for the living as a result.

Desperate to satisfy their hunger, the hungry ghosts eat rotten food or are forced to gorge on humiliating things such as vomit and feces.

Perhaps the most repugnant of the hungry ghosts are those condemned to feasting on human bodies. Known as jikininki in Japanese Buddhism, their eating habits are especially revolting. Take, for example, the tale a Buddhist priest told me in Japan about jikininki. Two jikininki were having dinner. One said, "You know, I really don't like Uncle Tetsu." The other replied, "Then just eat the noodles."

Ghost stories entertain and explain. They can be thrilling and thought-provoking; fun and foreboding.

The Petavatthu—a collection of 51 stories of preta—is part of the Buddhist scriptural tradition. Sometimes translated as "Stories of the Departed," the Petavatthu contains graphic accounts of those suffering from the negative consequences of their misdeeds in a previous life.

A common theme connecting many of the cautionary tales is the emphasis on the beneficial effects of being kind and generous; whereas those who are envious, jealous, miserly, greedy and ignorant are destined to a sorrowful existence as a preta. As punishment, preta are not only deprived of food, but clothing and dwelling as well. Fortunately for these condemned beings, preta can find release from their sufferings if their relatives perform meritorious deeds and share their merit with the preta. In one story, for example, a king saves a relative who was reborn as a preta by making generous offerings to the Buddha and his followers.

Some of the local Buddhist temples on the island can perform rituals—known as *osegaki*—that can appease the hunger of the preta and save them, too. Through osegaki, preta approach the temple and are offered specially blessed food in return for not causing mischief. In a sense, it's a Buddhist version of Halloween where the preta are the ones trick or treating. So this Halloween, enjoy the ghouls and goblins that visit your home, and be mindful of the preta that potentially exists within.

Buddha Day

When I was in elementary school, I believed in leprechauns and tooth fairies. I believed good people would always win and that God answered prayers. I also believed rabbits laid eggs. My world was wonderful and innocent. Yes, third grade was the best two years of my life.

I thought rabbits laid eggs because I saw Easter bunnies and baskets of eggs everywhere, especially during the spring. My world is different now and I no longer believe in many of the things I used to, but I still notice that chocolate rabbits and candy-filled eggs appear on the store shelves in the spring. There is something magical about the spring. Religions have noticed that too.

In the northern hemisphere, spring is a time when life and color return to the world after a winter of cold and darkness. I've come to learn that rabbits and brightly colored eggs—symbols of fertility and rebirth—signal this change.

One of the functions of religious holidays is to mark important events in the cycle of the year. Like rabbits and eggs, the religious holidays and festivals that occur in the spring celebrate the renewing power of light and life over darkness and death.

Holidays such as *Buddha Day* express the rhythmic changes of nature as well as communicate religious truths. Buddha Day celebrates the birth of the Buddha—whom Buddhists believe opened the path to enlightenment so that we might emerge from spiritual darkness and see with the light of understanding.

Buddhist tradition says the Buddha was born on the eighth day of the fourth month. Interestingly, not all Buddhist groups agree when that day is. In Hawai'i, some Buddhist groups celebrate the birth of the Buddha on the weekend nearest to April 8. Other groups follow a lunar calendar and therefore commemorate the occasion several weeks later. Buddhist tradition also designates Buddha Day as the most propitious time to bathe Buddha images and receive blessings in return.

According to Buddhist writings, Shakyamuni Buddha (the historical Buddha) was born in the garden at Lumbini in the northern part of India (currently Nepal). When Shakyamuni was born, heavenly music played, birds sang, flowers bloomed and fell from the sky, and sweet dew fell from heaven to bathe the baby Buddha. The infant then took seven steps, and with his right hand pointing to heaven above (symbolizing the eternal) and left hand pointing to earth below (symbolizing the transient), declared that this would be his last rebirth. He would break free from *samsara*—the continuous cycle of death and rebirth—as he was destined to become the Enlightened One and lead humanity out of suffering. The Buddha would go on to live for 80 years, helping all kinds of people through his teachings.

This story is celebrated in various ways at the many local Buddhist temples in Hawai'i, though bathing Buddha images, adorning altars with flowers reminiscent of Lumbini garden, and creating lantern displays to express the enlightenment offered by the Buddha to the world are common themes. These practices are also done with the hope that followers may have long and healthy lives, blessings, and the fulfillment of wishes.

Rituals are performed at certain junctures of the year to make those occasions meaningful. The festival celebrating the birth of the Buddha occurs in the spring at roughly the same time as the Jewish festival of Passover—when God led the enslaved Israelites out of captivity—and the Christian celebration of Easter—which commemorates the resurrection of Christ. Notions of purification, a new beginning, and liberation from spiritual bondage are central themes in these religious holidays. Observing the holidays allows believers to reconnect to these experiences. In this sense the holidays do not change the seasons, but can change those who participate in them. The rituals associated with these holidays give us the opportunity to renew ourselves and see again with child-like eyes a world full of wonder, even though we are no longer in the third grade.

Obon

The Obon festival in Hawai'i is an invented tradition. It is the Spam musubi of Buddhism. It has its origins elsewhere, but it is reshaped, repackaged, and resold here. It is a popular social and cultural event wrapped in religious motifs that add poignancy and perhaps legitimacy to the whole affair. It ties traditional Buddhist practices inside the temple with decidedly non-Buddhist ones outside. Indeed, many come to the Buddhist temples during Obon to enjoy the food, games, homemade goods, and unconventional songs and dances that have little or nothing to do with Buddhism, unless of course the dance movements to Electric Slide or Tanko Bushi are expressions of enlightenment. At the Bon Dances Buddhism is not necessary to enjoy this Buddhist tradition.

Obon only lasts a few days in Japan. In Hawai'i, Obon has been reshaped to last all summer long. (The Ullambana Sutra, the scriptural basis for Obon, specifies only one day—the 15th day of the 7th month—as the day of observance. However, the sutra itself is an invented tradition, as it was not produced in India during the time of the Buddha, but created many centuries later in China.) The Obon season in Hawai'i unofficially began with the hugely successful Memorial Day lantern floating ceremony at Ala Moana Beach Park. This was odd on several levels.

One, the lantern floating ceremony is traditionally observed at the end of the Obon season, not at the beginning. In the Buddhist tradition, Obon is a time for communities to rejoice, reflect, and express gratitude to our ancestors and welcome their spirits back to this world with gifts of food and other offerings. The Bon Dance is understood as part of the celebration of this reunion. The lantern floating ceremony thus concludes the reunion by guiding the spirits back to the other world until the following year. The Memorial Day lantern floating ceremony—repackaged so that it is observed before the traditional start of the Obon festival and before the first Bon Dance is held—sends the spirits back to the other world before they've even had the chance to arrive. This seems rude.

Two, Memorial Day is a national holiday that pays homage to those in the United States Armed Forces who gave their lives in service for their country. The lantern floating ceremony, by contrast, resells the holiday as a time to offer prayers for all spirits, "even endemic, endangered and extinct plant and animal life." (*lanternfloatinghawaii.com*) By extending the honor reserved for those who died in military service to all ancestors from all cultures in all traditions—religious and otherwise, human and non-human alike—does the lantern floating ceremony embrace the meaning of Memorial Day or dilute it?

Three, the tradition of one culture (Memorial Day) is mixed with the tradition of another (Obon) to create something different (lantern floating ceremony) under the guise of something traditional (universal peace and harmony) that ultimately gives prominence to something new (Shinnyo-en). The sponsor of the Memorial Day lantern floating ceremony is Shinnyo-en, a Japanese new religion founded in 1936. Scholars view Shinnyo-en as a new religion in part because it has unconventional, if not innovative, beliefs and practices: believers venerate a deceased Japanese man and his family (the current leader is his daughter and followers believe his two sons willingly died in childhood as sacrifices for the faith), ordinary followers may become spiritual mediums after several years of training, and the sect is adept at utilizing contemporary practices that garner public attention—indeed, the lantern floating ceremony is a public relations boon for the religion. In other words, Shinnyo-en is skilled at inventing tradition.

This is not necessarily a bad thing. Traditions are not meant to be stagnant. Traditions are meant to provide continuity and are enriched by contributions from diverse sources. In short, traditions change. Standing tradition is thus an oxymoron. A floating tradition, however, is not.

Though the festival has its origins in Buddhism, the themes that characterize Obon and the lantern floating ceremony are neither uniquely Buddhist nor particularly Japanese. The layers of meaning that inform the Obon festival are shaped and tied by different people from different backgrounds and blend sentiments that resonate in various cultural and religious traditions, invented and otherwise.

Buddhism & Violence

My wife is a pretend Buddhist. She claims to be Buddhist, but she doesn't spend her days memorizing passages from any of the sutras. She has other things to do. My wife doesn't know the names of the different Buddhist figures enshrined at the various temples, but she shows respect and offers prayers at the various places of worship she visits. Despite not knowing much of its history or writings, she maintains Buddhism is about compassion, not killing. Compassionate killing in Buddhism is a contradiction in terms.

Most people assume Buddhism is intimately associated with peace. There is indeed a close connection between Buddhism and peace, as the first precept in Buddhism prohibits killing or causing harm. But like other faiths, there is a darker, violent side to the religion as well. Why is this? Because people have a darker, violent side and this is expressed through and satisfied in religion. The religions aren't violent; people are. And, in some cases, the Buddha is too.

The Upayakausalya (Skill in Means) Sutra tells the story of a past life of the Buddha, where he is captain of a boat carrying five hundred merchants. In a dream one night, deities inform him that one of the passengers is a bandit who is planning to kill all the merchants. The Buddha considers three possible actions: do nothing and allow the bandit to kill everyone; inform the merchants, who would then kill the bandit themselves and incur evil karma for their murder as a result; or kill the bandit himself. The Buddha ponders this ethical dilemma for several days, and eventually decides to murder the bandit himself. The sutra does not interpret this as retribution for evil, but as an act of compassion that saves the bandit from the horrible karmic consequences of mass murder, and allows the bandit to be reborn in heaven. A distinction is made between allowing the merchants to kill the bandit in anger, which would result in their rebirth in hell, and the Buddha's murder with "great compassion" and "skillful means" which saves everyone.

Compassion and proper understanding are central to achieving Buddhahood, and the tale of the Buddha, the bandit, and the merchants underscores this. Under certain circumstances, violence may be performed by spiritually adept beings, but not by ordinary beings. This is an expression (misinterpretation?) of the Buddhist theory of two truths—conventional truth, which frames a reality filled with diverse and distinctive things and beings; and ultimate truth, the view that there are no distinctive things or beings, but an underlying interconnectedness between everything, including the two truths. Enlightened beings or those with proper understanding of the higher truth transcend the ordinary ethical norms that characterize conventional levels of morality. In short, violence is justifiable when performed by the Buddhas and Buddhists, but condemned when committed by non-Buddhists. This in part explains the Buddhist complicity in wars throughout Asian history. Indeed, in recent years Buddhist monks have incited violence and attacked Muslims in Myanmar under the guise of peace.

There is an ethical double standard here. Behavior that is normally condemned—particularly when committed by people of other religious or ethnic groups—is justified when performed by people belonging to one's own group. The ethical double standard applies to other religions too. "Thou shalt not kill" in the Ten Commandments prohibits the killing of God's people. The murder of other people—including children and infants—is acceptable. In fact, in certain books in the Bible God demands it (1 Samuel 15, Deuteronomy 7). One can easily find examples in Islam, too (Surah 2:191-193, Surah 8:12). The messy interplay between the purity of religious ideals on the one hand and the sometime violent field of social practice on the other is not easy to manage, and every world religion struggles with this.

My wife denies Buddhists can practice their faith and be violent. In this way she is like my Muslim friends who claim the Quran is misread when used to justify violence. Or like my Christian friends who claim Jesus only preached tolerance and family values. A closer look at their religious traditions would reveal otherwise. There is no hypocrisy here, though. When it comes to committing violent acts or hateful behavior, decent people of religious faith are either unaware of the violent and appalling passages in their scriptural tradition or know them but—thankfully—reinterpret them or reject them outright. Decent people are still peaceful and tolerant, even when strands within their religious traditions encourage them to be otherwise.

Upstanding people don't need to be Buddhist—or Christian, Muslim, Hindu, or atheist, for that matter. They don't need labels at all. My wife respects the faith of others (though some do not respect hers in return). She is a decent person and a pretend Buddhist. The world should be filled with religious pretenders. Perhaps the world already is.

The Buddha Is A Musubi

The Buddha is a musubi. At least that is the image that comes to mind when I think of the enlightened one sitting in meditation under the Bodhi tree. With legs crossed and hands placed on his lap one on the other, the seated figure is a musubi-like triangle shape. A robe wraps around his body like a piece of nori. Eyes half-closed with an ever so subtle smile on his lips, it's difficult to know what he is thinking about. Like the filling inside a musubi hidden from plain view, the emphasis of the seated Buddha is what we can't fully see—the mind within. But what's on the inside is as important as what is on the outside.

Moreover, just as there are basically three essential parts to the musubi—rice, filling and nori—there are three interconnecting sides to Buddhism known as the Three Jewels: Buddha, Dharma, Sangha. I think of the Buddha as the rice; the Dharma (teachings) as the filling; and the Sangha (community of followers) as the nori.

There are different kinds of rice in different places. Buddhism is like this, too. Buddhism began in India in the fifth century BCE, but achieved greater success beyond its birthplace when it traveled to Sri Lanka, China, Southeast Asia, Korea, Japan, Tibet and elsewhere. Moreover, wherever Buddhism traveled to, the religion interacted with the local culture and indigenous religious tradition, creating new and distinctive forms of Buddhism in each place. Sort of like the musubi. Musubi in Hawai'i has changed into something different from what it was in Japan.

To begin with, what we in Hawai'i know as *musubi* is referred to as *omusubi* in parts of Japan. The "o" in front of "musubi" is an honorific prefix in Japanese. We don't show the musubi the same level of respect in Hawai'i. We disregard the traditional Japanese shapes of the omusubi—round, triangular, or cylindrical—and turn out rectangle rice bricks instead. We even split the musubi into two, making it almost like a rice sandwich. We don't use Japanese short grain rice, but use medium grain rice or whatever is on sale.

The traditional Japanese omusubi is often nearly engulfed by nori, with only snippets of rice peeping out of the corners. The good stuff—ume, salmon, konbu and other filling—is kept enclosed and hidden. The traditional Japanese omusubi is reserved and subtle. Like Buddhism.

The local spam musubi, on the other hand, is bold and brash. It reminds me of Christ crucified, or least in the way that he is depicted in some churches—with his body and passion exposed for all to see. Only a loincloth provides him with a degree of modesty. The meaty spam too, in all its cholesterol busting, saturated fat and sodium-laden glory reclines unabashedly on the top of a block of rice, held in place by a nori thong. It is unrepentant and mocks our efforts to eat healthy, like the criminal hanging next to Christ who ridiculed the savior's innocence.

If sexy is what you hide and pornography is what you expose and exploit, the Japanese omusubi is sexy while the local spam version is musubi porn.

And yet, perhaps it's time for local Buddhist groups interested in widening their appeal to look to the spam musubi for insight and guidance. Like the spam musubi, Buddhist groups might consider changing their shape into something local people can easily form on their own. And instead of subtly placing delicacies in the middle of the musubi where it is easily hidden from view, place the good stuff on the outside for everyone to see. In other words, transform fillings into toppings.

This may already be happening in some Buddhist groups. In the past, the Buddhist teaching of emptiness was difficult to fathom except by those with profound understanding inside the religion. Emptiness is now being filled with mindfulness. What is more, mindfulness is being moved to the forefront of the religion for all to see. The Buddhist practice of mindfulness is now tied to all sorts of products and has become an effective marketing tool that has opened Buddhism to those outside the religion not familiar with its traditional forms. In short, the omusubi is becoming its spam version.

Yet even the musubi has an expiration date. It needs to be consumed and more need to be produced, perhaps with different fillings or toppings. The spam musubi is evolving, too. I've seen an over-the-top spam/bacon/egg/avocado musubi. The nori strains to contain this obese musubi, like the waistband of underwear too small that hides and exposes at the same time. Perhaps Buddhism has an expiration date, too. Maybe newer forms filled or topped with local favorites will be created, causing some Buddhists to blush and others to leer.

Chinese, Korean and Japanese Buddhism

When our daughter was only a few months old, my wife and I took her grocery shopping with us in Hawaiʻi Kai. We were new parents proudly walking down the aisles when a woman stopped us to compliment us on our daughter. "My, what a lovely baby. What race is she?" I proudly replied, "Well, I'm Japanese, and my wife is Chinese." "Oh, so she's Korean?" the woman laughed and walked away, pleased with herself.

It is difficult to tell Chinese, Koreans, and Japanese apart. To many people, they all look the same. For Chinese, Korean, and Japanese Buddhists, however, this is certainly not the case. As Buddhism spread from its origins in India to China, Korea, and Japan, it adapted to and blended with the native religious traditions of each culture, resulting in several different and very distinctive forms of Buddhism.

There are thus recognizable traits and characteristics at Chinese, Korean, and Japanese Buddhist temples that distinguish one from the other. Here's a brief guide for helping visitors to local Buddhist temples discern which is which:

Chinese Temples

The Confucian emphasis on ancestor veneration and Daoist influence on divination practices are prominent at local Chinese Buddhist temples. Before even entering the temple grounds, one notices Chinese temples often are painted in colors representing the five elements: red, yellow, green, black and white. The colors symbolize certain values, including balance, harmony, and prosperity. Inside the temple gate area, but just outside the entrance of the temple itself, one will often see followers burning paper offerings in the form of spirit money, clothes, houses, and other goods, and sending these to the ancestors. The offerings are a way to maintain relationships with the deceased. Within the temples, there are cushions on the ground for followers to kneel on when praying and consulting the gods. One will also see followers pull sticks of bamboo from a canister, then throw red moon blocks on the floor to divine guidance from the gods.

These traits and practices are not found at Korean or Japanese temples.

Korean Temples

It is easy to recognize Korean Buddhist temples by the distinctive and traditional decorative coloring known as dancheong. Dancheong (literally "red-blue") is painted onto the eaves of the temple's roof and is distinguished by its fascinating patterns of animals (dragons, lions, cranes), flowers, and geometric designs. Dancheong enhances the spiritual quality of the temple and some believe it protects the temple and its followers. The eaves of Chinese and Japanese temples, by contrast, are plain.

Most Korean Buddhist temples will also have a shrine in the back of the temple dedicated to the spirit of the mountain deity (sanshin-gak), though sometimes the deity (usually depicted as an old man accompanied by a tiger) is venerated in a painting within one of the main worship halls.

Mu Ryang-sa is the largest Korean Buddhist temple on the island. I was repeatedly told during several visits that sanshin-gak was a form of folk superstition thus the practice was not observed at Mu Ryang-sa. I was ready to give up the idea that sanshin-gak was an integral part of Korean Buddhism when a woman at the temple whispered to me: "I'll show you sanshin-gak." She led me to one of the worship halls and showed me a painting with numerous mythical figures. "See sanshin?" I didn't. "Look carefully at the top, left side." There was a picture of Pele, the local mountain deity. Mu Ryang-sa is a traditional Korean temple after all.

Japanese Temples

When Buddhism arrived in Japan in 538 CE, it interacted with the native religious tradition—Shinto—and each influenced the other. Among the several values and themes present in Shinto, its emphasis on purity and nature is most prominent at Japanese Buddhist temples. Japanese Buddhist temples tend not to be as richly painted or decorated as its Chinese and Korean counterparts. Indeed, it is common in Japan for the temples to be plain colored or left unpainted—the wood used to build the temples left in its natural state. Another distinctive feature of Japanese religion is the practice of physically and spiritually cleansing oneself before entering the temple. A washbasin is commonly found outside temples and shrines for followers to wash their hands and rinse their mouths. The emphasis on purity extends to inside the temple, where the floor, walls, and altar area are immaculately cleaned and wiped. This is in stark contrast to Chinese Buddhist temples where dust and incense ashes are scattered about. For Japanese Buddhists this is unacceptable and a sign of disrespect. For Chinese Buddhists, the dust and ash symbolize the presence of the power of the Buddhas. Wiping them away renders the temple sterile and impotent.

All of this—the emphasis on divination and ancestor veneration, the importance of revering local mountain deities and temple painting designs with spiritual power, and the emphasis on the pure and natural—encompasses the values and traits that characterize Chinese, Korean, and Japanese cultures and distinguishes one Buddhist temple from another. The gods and Buddhas know not all Asians are alike, even if some people don't.

Tibetan Buddhism

Buddhism is a made up religion. This ability to reinvent itself has played an important role in the successful spread of Buddhism. While some religions are still associated with one particular ethnic group or a specific geographical location, Buddhism has transcended such boundaries. What is more, whereas other religions have spread aggressively by force—physical and/or theological—Buddhism has largely cultivated for itself a positive reputation for peace and compassion wherever it has traveled. It has been able to achieve this for the most part because Buddhism has effectively recreated itself to adjust to the local context wherever it has spread. Tibetan Buddhism is a case in point.

There are certain traits in Tibetan Buddhism that distinguish it from most other forms of Buddhism. To begin with, Buddhism arrived in Tibet rather late when compared to the acceptance of Buddhism in other countries. Buddhism began in India in the fifth century BCE, but did not reach Tibet until roughly 1,000 years later in the seventh century CE. By this time Buddhism had already established itself elsewhere—Sri Lanka, China, Southeast Asia, Korea, and Japan—centuries before. Buddhism entered Tibet from India a second time in the eleventh century, introducing yet another form of Buddhism that interacted with the local culture and indigenous religious tradition.

Tibetan Buddhism is largely based on different scriptures from the ones that influenced Buddhism in places such as China, Korea, and Japan. In those countries, Buddhist sutras became highly influential whereas in Tibet, other writings, including Buddhist tantras, shaped the religion. Buddhist tantras—intimately connected to esoteric Buddhism—developed in India in the sixth or seventh century CE, long after the time of the historical Buddha. The writings of tantric Buddhism are based on the notion that progress in the path to enlightenment may be hastened through techniques of esoteric ritual and yoga. In tantric Buddhism, the sacred is realized in the ordinary, and the adept can transcend worldly desires by fulfilling them. Spiritually accomplished teachers—known as *lamas*—reveal these esoteric teachings and practices to qualified disciples.

Lamas are highly revered religious figures in Tibetan Buddhism and followers give them absolute faith and loyalty. As various Buddhist sects and monasteries in Tibet gained power, the leading lamas also began to wield significant authority, both political and spiritual. However, since many of the lamas took vows of celibacy, problems of succession arose. A response to this issue was the rise of the unique Tibetan Buddhist practice of belief in a reincarnate lama. After the death of a great lama, religious elders began a search to identify the next incarnation of the spiritual master. This practice was developed in Tibet in the eleventh century and there are about 3,000 lines of incarnation of various lamas.

Luckily for Tibetan Buddhists and the search committee, the departed spirits of the lamas have tended to be reincarnated in Tibet. While there are numerous lamas in Tibetan Buddhism, the best known is the world famous Dalai Lama.

The title "Dalai Lama" (Ocean of Wisdom) was created by a Mongolian ruler in the 16th century and bestowed upon a high-ranking lama in one of the Tibetan Buddhist sects. However, the first Dalai Lama to assume political and spiritual leadership of Tibet was the 5th Dalai Lama. This occurred in 1642 after defeating political and religious rivals—including those of other Tibetan Buddhist sects. From then until 1959, when a revolt broke out against Chinese control of the region, Tibet was ruled by a succession of Dalai Lamas, each male and each identified as a young child after his predecessor had died. The 14th (and current) Dalai Lama escaped to India during the revolt where he led a government in exile. China rejects this government.

The second highest-ranking lama—known as the Panchen Lama— plays a significant role in identifying the next Dalai Lama. In turn, the Dalai Lama selects the future Panchen Lama. After the death of the 10th Panchen Lama in 1989, the current Dalai Lama recognized a child in Tibet as the 11th incarnation. China rejected this selection—as control of the Panchen Lama can lead to control of the Dalai Lama—and chose a different boy instead. Chinese authorities removed the Dalai Lama's choice and the boy has not been seen since.

Persecuting religion usually does not weaken it, but invigorates it. China's attempt to repress Tibetan Buddhism has caused the religion to flourish elsewhere, including in the United States, where it is reinventing itself yet again to appeal to the wider public. The esoteric rituals central to Tibetan Buddhism designed to appease spirits and bring about good luck are downplayed or neglected altogether. Instead an emphasis on Tibetan Buddhism as a mystical tradition that stresses meditation and logic characterizes the American version of the religion. Reverence for the Dalai Lama, however, remains constant.

In 2011, the Dalai Lama made a shrewd political move by divesting himself of political power. The Dalai Lama has also suggested that he might be reincarnated as a woman or indeed not be reincarnated at all after his death. Such is the privilege that comes with enlightenment to determine one's own post-mortem fate. The Dalai Lama's actions have infuriated the Chinese government as it nullifies the importance of the Chinese selected Panchen Lama. Many Tibetans, who seek to preserve cherished traditions in their political and spiritual struggle with China are also troubled by these developments. The institution of the Dalai Lama is man-made, however. Its demise might also be the same as Tibetan Buddhism reinvents itself to continue outside Tibet.

American Buddhism

I trained as a Buddhist minister for 2 years—and then I got married. And although that was quite a while ago, I am still invited to participate in discussions concerning the future of Buddhism in Hawai'i and comment on the emergence of an American form of Buddhism.

What has impacted the development of Buddhism in the United States and what will influence its rate of growth? In my view, three factors—all beginning with the letter C for the sake of convenience—shape the character traits of American Buddhism: Christianity, the Constitution, and Consumerism.

Christianity

Wherever Buddhism has traveled, Buddhism has changed to accommodate the local customs and religious traditions it has encountered. This explains in part why Thai Buddhism is different from Tibetan Buddhism, and why both differ from Japanese Buddhism. The same applies to American Buddhism.

Christianity is the predominate religion in the United States. And in order for American Buddhism to develop, Buddhists have largely adopted two strategies to spread their faith in the United States, both of which take into account the influential presence of Christianity. The first strategy is to boldly characterize Buddhism as an alternate religion to Christianity. Buddhism is promoted as a religion that openly teaches the acceptance of change and diversity while emphasizing non-violence and compassion for all beings (as opposed to an absolute insistence on one eternal truth and certain condemnation of those who reject this truth). The second, more subtle and more common strategy is to claim that Buddhism is not a religion at all, but a meditational way of life. Meditation cultivates mindfulness and the concomitant moral and ethical virtues, such as compassion and generosity that lead to an enriching and fulfilling life. Here, Buddhists shift the focus of Buddhism away from a traditional religion to a contemporary means of being fully awake and mindful of the world around us and of the world within us. By this strategy, Buddhism is not a rival to Christianity. In fact, one can practice the Buddhist lifestyle and still be Christian.

Constitution

The majority of Buddhists in the world do not practice meditation. Meditation is something best left to the experts: monks, nuns, and priests. Indeed, priests, monks and nuns play a vital role in the majority of places where Buddhism is practiced. They preserve and promote the teachings of the Buddha and perform rituals for the well-being of the country and its people. It's different in American Buddhism.

The equal protection clause in the 14th Amendment to the US Constitution proclaims that states must treat all its citizens equally. This echoes the Declaration of Independence, which famously declares, "We hold these truths to be self evident, that all men are created equal."

Thus in American Buddhism, the function and need for priests, monks, and nuns are reduced, as ordinary Buddhists believe they are fully capable of interpreting the Buddha's teachings for themselves and anyone can practice meditation, not just the elite. One does not need to take the vows of a monk or nun or don their robes to do so. This egalitarian ideal accounts for the numerous lay-led Buddhist groups in America.

Consumerism

The First Amendment to the US Constitution prohibits the government from favoring one particular religion over any other. All religions are equal in the eyes of the law. As a result, religions in the United States compete for members. This explains in part why two of the most well-known Christian groups that proselytize—Mormons and Jehovah's Witnesses—are American forms of Christianity. It also explains why at many local churches a service is barely over before worshippers are bombarded with invitations to purchase church products.

Buddhists have begun to emulate the marketing practices of their Christian counterparts by transforming their spiritual message into consumable products. *Mindfulness* is the preeminent example here. American Buddhism has skillfully utilized the term and concept of mindfulness to introduce and popularize Buddhist and Buddhist-inspired ideas and practices.

There is a host of goods and services that promote mindfulness (which in turn opens a path for Buddhism to gain wider acceptance in popular culture). There are countless books and products on mindful ways of doing things--eating, parenting, money management, sex, politics, sports, dealing with illness, etc. Whatever it is you desire, there is a mindful way of achieving it.

Some may argue that mindfulness is the fundamental practice found in early and "true" Buddhism. Perhaps. But from the earliest times (and even today here in Hawai'i), Buddhist monks and nuns cultivated mindfulness as a path towards enlightenment and as a means to sever attachment to the values of a transient world. In the United States, however, American Buddhism is not a religion that transcends the desires of world; but a mindful way of consuming them.

ON CHRISTIANITY

Christianities I

The question comes up in one form or another in my religion classes: Are Catholics Christian? Yes, they are. Not only are Catholics Christian, but Catholic Christianity is one of the oldest (if not the oldest) forms of Christianity. The Catholic Church traces itself back to Peter, who was one of Jesus' most prominent disciples. What is more, according to tradition Peter became the first pope. Why, then, do some accuse Catholics of not being Christian?

There has never been a single form of Christianity. The apostles of Christ themselves argued over what it meant to be Christian. Paul's conflict with Peter—where the former openly opposed the latter and charged him with hypocrisy (Galatians 2:11-14)—is an example of this disagreement. Currently, there are thousands of types of Christianities, but most of these are associated (however loosely) with one of three major forms: Catholic Christianity, Orthodox Christianity, and Protestant Christianity. Churches representing all three forms can be found in Hawai'i and I strongly recommend visiting all three types—especially if you consider yourself a Christian—to gain a deeper understanding of Christianity.

The three major forms of Christianity have battled one another—physically, verbally, and theologically—multiple times in history and, as Paul did to Peter, openly opposed each other and leveled charges of hypocrisy with such intensity that even today there is lasting unease and conflict between the three branches. One of the results of these lingering sentiments between the three groups is the notion that one form of Christianity is more authentic than the others. Or to put the matter in another way, other forms of Christianity different from one's own are not genuinely Christian.

While it would take more than a single article to delineate the differences between Catholic, Orthodox, and Protestant Christianities, here are a few distinctions:

Catholics, Orthodox, and Protestants look to different earthly authorities for spiritual guidance. The pope leads the Catholic Church and in the view of Catholics, the pope's authority is perfect and divinely sanctioned. In the Gospel of Matthew (16:18-19), Jesus gives the keys to heaven to Peter. Jesus also tells Peter that he (Jesus) will build his church on him (Peter). As a result, Catholics believe the pope is the foundation of the church and the pope has the authority to decide who gets into heaven and who does not. This explains in part why Catholics confess their sins to a priest—the priests represent the pope thus they hold the keys to the kingdom.

The Orthodox Church is one of the oldest (if not the oldest) forms of Christianity (Orthodox and Catholic Christians disagree which church is older). The Orthodox Church traces itself back to the apostle Andrew, Peter's brother. Orthodox Christians reject the authority of the pope and look to a patriarch for guidance instead. According to the Gospel of John (1:40-42), it was Andrew who found Jesus first and subsequently brought his brother Peter to Jesus. In other words, if it weren't for Andrew (Orthodox Christianity), Peter (Catholic Christianity) would not have met Christ. Peter (pope) thus has little right to assert his authority over Andrew (patriarch).

Disputes over the reach of authority each church leader had and how theological issues were shaped as a consequence resulted in the pope excommunicating the patriarch and vice-versa. A formal split between the two churches occurred in 1054. War followed not long afterwards. The divide hardened the different paths of development each church followed, leading to significant disparities in beliefs and practices. For example, Catholics and Orthodox Christians do not agree on how to observe the most sacred of all Christian rituals—the Eucharist—and the two churches follow different calendars, resulting in disagreement over when to celebrate Christmas and Easter, the two most important holidays in Christianity.

Protestant Christianity refers to a vast collection of assorted churches and Christian groups that number in the thousands. These churches are so diverse and different from one another in beliefs and practices that the only thing they have in common is their agreement that they are not Catholic or Orthodox.

Protestant Christianity cannot claim to be the oldest form of Christianity—indeed it appears late in history, 1500 years after the death of Jesus. Instead, Protestant churches claim to be the truest form of Christianity, arguing that the Orthodox and Catholic churches have gone astray from the teachings of Christ because they are led by men and influenced by beliefs and practices not based on the Bible. The Bible, then, is the primary source of religious authority for Protestant Christianity. This may seem straightforward, but it isn't.

Those who claim the Bible is the true word of God are often unaware that different Christians use different Bibles. They are under the impression that the Bible is the same for everyone—containing the exact same books and the exact same message. Nothing could be further from the truth. Different Bibles have different books and different teachings. I'll explain how this can be in the next article.

Christianities II

I can usually tell the Protestant Christians in my classes. They are the ones who have Bible verses memorized and want to preface and end their statements (and everything in between) with scriptural passages. This is in stark contrast to my Catholic Christian students, who admit, "Well, I *should* read the Bible, but…" Their admission is the result of a history in the Catholic Church of ordinary Christians not reading the Bible because they couldn't—Latin was the designated language of the Catholic Bible and many Catholic Christians could not read in their own native language, much less in Latin; and there was no need to—they have a perfect spiritual leader (the pope) to guide them.

Protestant Christians were largely responsible for translating the Bible into the native languages of various peoples, rendering the Bible accessible and understandable to ordinary Christians. Prior to this, Latin (Catholic Church) and Greek (Orthodox Church) were the primary languages of the Christian Bible.

Enabling ordinary Christians to read the Bible on their own has had several consequences. On the positive side, this encourages Protestant Christians to be knowledgeable and responsible about their scriptural tradition. On the negative side, encouraging Protestant Christians to interpret the Bible for themselves has led to wacky (and sometimes dangerous) groups with extremist beliefs.

But the Bible has never been a single, unalterable unit sent down from heaven. It has been changed over time and altered to conform to and support the beliefs of the churches. This accounts for the numerous translations of the Bible available.

For example, the only passage in the Christian Bible that explicitly affirms the doctrine of the trinity is what is known as the *Johannine Comma*—so called because it is a short phrase found in a writing attributed to Jesus' disciple John. Mention of the Father, Son, and Holy Spirit can be found elsewhere in the Christian Bible, but only 1 John 5:7-8 unequivocally states, "and these three are one." The problem is that the *Johannine Comma* is not in the earliest and best Bible manuscripts. The passage was created later—centuries after the death of Jesus' disciples—and inserted into the Bible, where it still exists in various forms in many (but not in all) translations. A survey of the different Bible translations bears this out. This problematic passage explains in part why different Christian churches hold different views regarding the Holy Trinity, some even going so far as to reject the doctrine altogether.

In short, different Christian groups use different Bibles. Orthodox Christians have 76 books in their Bible, Catholic Christians have 73 books in theirs, and Protestant Christians have 66 books. In the 16th century, Martin Luther and other Protestant Christians deleted several books from the Bible, including Maccabees, *Tobit, Esdras, Judith, Wisdom of Solomon, Ecclesiasticus, Baruch,* and other writings. (Atheists probably wish he didn't stop there.) Protestant Christians rejected these books because they were written in Greek and not in Hebrew, the original language of the Bible. Interestingly, however, the entire New Testament was written in Greek though it wasn't the language of Jesus, either. Luther and his supporters also sought to remove *Hebrews, James, Jude* and the *Book of Revelation* from the Bible because they contradicted what he considered to be Protestant teachings. Alas he was unsuccessful in removing them.

The biblical books that the Protestants did remove were important writings for the Catholic Church as they contained the underpinnings for its teachings on purgatory, prayers for the dead, and the intercession of saints. As a result, Protestants reject these Catholic ideas as unbiblical. This is behind the Protestant charge that Catholics are not Christian because they observe beliefs and practices not found in the Bible. Yes, they are unbiblical from a Protestant perspective because they are not in *their* Bible—the Protestant Bible.

In the Protestant view, the Church should be based on the Bible; from the Catholic and Orthodox perspectives however, it's the other way around: the Bible is the product of the Church and the Bible supports the Church. The closing to John's Gospel (21:25) reads: *But there are also many other things that Jesus did; if every one of them were written down, I suppose that the world itself could not contain the books that would be written.* In other words, the Bible does not tell us everything Jesus said and did. Could Lent, infant baptism, and the veneration of saints be a part of this unwritten tradition kept by the followers of Christ? Catholic and Orthodox Christians believe so.

Not only do different Christian churches use different Bibles, but even the books within the same Bible differ from each other, some to such an extent that they produce contradictions. For example, the gospels do not agree when Jesus died (was it before or after Passover?), what he taught (was it only one truth or many truths?), or how he taught (only through parables or without parables at all?). These discrepancies account for the different and sometimes incompatible teachings and practices between the Orthodox, Catholic, and Protestant churches. What exactly these differences and contradictions are and the consequences such disparities produced I will discuss in the next article.

Christianities III

I n previous columns, I tried to delineate some of the differences between the three major forms of Christianity: Catholic, Orthodox, and Protestant. I conclude here with a look at the various interpretations of the most sacred Christian ritual—the Eucharist.

Also known by other names—including Holy Communion and Lord's Supper—the Eucharist commemorates the Last Supper, when Christ and his disciples shared bread and wine. During this meal, Christ equated the bread and wine with his own flesh and blood that would serve as an offering for the sins of humanity. In other words, the Eucharist is where the sins of humanity meet the forgiveness of God. Those who are denied the Eucharist, therefore, are denied the forgiveness of sins. In general, only those who have confessed faith in Christ are allowed to participate in the Eucharist.

The overwhelming majority of Christian churches observe the Eucharist in some fashion. They may not all agree on exactly what it means, or how to observe it, or how often to observe it, but in general they agree it is the foundation of their faith: the sacrifice of Christ for the sins of the world.

Part of the reason for the disagreement between Christian churches regarding the Eucharist is the gospels themselves don't agree when Jesus died. In short, the gospels contradict each other when it comes to the most important Christian ritual.

According to the Gospel of Mark (Matthew and Luke too, since in the view of scholars they copied Mark), Jesus was crucified the morning *after*

Passover. The Last Supper Christ had with his disciples, therefore, was the Passover meal. Passover is a Jewish holiday that commemorates the Exodus, when God—through Moses—led his people out of spiritual bondage in Egypt. During Passover, Jews eat unleavened bread, which means that when Jesus said the bread was his body, he meant unleavened bread. This explains why Catholics and most Protestants use unleavened bread for their Eucharist.

Orthodox Christians, however, follow the Gospel of John. The Gospel of John states Jesus died at about noon on the day *before* Passover. This is one day earlier than what the other gospels say. This means the Last Supper Jesus had with his disciples was not the Passover meal. And if it was not Passover, the bread eaten was leavened bread, not unleavened. For this reason, Orthodox Christians celebrate the Eucharist with leavened bread, not the cracker-like wafer used in Catholic and many Protestant churches.

Because John has Jesus dying when the Passover meal was being prepared, only John's Gospel calls Jesus the "lamb of God" and the "bread of life" and the "true vine." Jews have bread, lamb, and wine, among other foods, during Passover. For John, Jesus' death symbolized the new Passover meal. Matthew, Mark, and Luke do not refer to Jesus as "lamb of God," "bread of life," or "true vine." It wouldn't make much sense to do so, since these gospels have Jesus dying when the Passover meal was already finished.

One may wonder why the bother with what kind of bread to use for the Eucharist? It matters. (Indeed, religious wars have been waged over the issue.) For Orthodox and Catholic Christians, the wine is not just wine and the bread is not simply bread. The wine is the actual blood of Christ and the bread is his literal body. It matters therefore which type of bread Jesus meant when he said, "This is my body." Was it leavened or unleavened bread? To get the bread wrong is to miss out on Christ. Put another way, only one group of Christians is really eating Jesus; the other is simply having a snack.

As I mentioned in a previous column on the different kinds of Christianities, Protestant Christianity refers to a large and diverse collection of Christian groups that share little in common except for the fact that they are not Orthodox or Catholic. Some interpret the Bible literally, others take a symbolic approach; some believe Christ is actually present in the bread and wine (Episcopalians, Lutherans), but most Protestant Christians believe the presence of Christ is symbolic. Because most Protestant Christians believe the bread and wine are not the actual flesh and blood of Christ, but symbolize them instead, actual wine need not be used for the ritual. Grape juice or even water can be substituted. (Interestingly, many Protestant Christians interpret the Bible literally except when it comes to the Eucharist.)

In conclusion, many are familiar with the Christian insistence that there is only one truth and only one way to it. Yet the sheer number of different forms of Christianities and different beliefs and different practices and even different Bibles tells us otherwise. Who, then, are the true Christians? Ultimately only God knows, but I'd place my bet on the ones who are kind, accepting, and forgiving, regardless of which church they belong to or indeed, regardless of whether or not they go to church at all. Those who write nasty emails to me are probably Christians of a different sort.

How To Get To Heaven

A student visited me in my office with a personal question. She had recently lost her beloved grandmother and wanted to know what happened to her after her death. She wanted to know specifically if her grandmother was in hell. I asked why would she even think something like that? She said it was what her friends had told her—that because her grandmother had been Buddhist and did not accept Jesus Christ as her personal lord and savior, she was in hell. She wanted to know if this was true. I told her she should change friends. Anyone who says such hateful things and cares more about his or her own faith than the sadness of a grieving friend is not a friend. She was persistent and wanted to know if the Bible indeed says what her friends told her. I told her the Bible says lots of things, and that when people quote the Bible they are telling you more about what's in their hearts rather than what the Bible says. Not satisfied, she wanted to know if there was a specific passage for her grandmother, one that says a person could go to heaven even if one isn't Christian. Yes, there is.

According to what Jesus says in Matthew 25:31-46, belief in Jesus is not required for eternal life. In fact, this passage makes it clear that it is not even necessary to know Jesus to inherit the kingdom of heaven. One is rewarded with eternal life based on whether or not one feeds the hungry, clothes the naked, takes care of the sick, and visits those in prison. This theme is echoed elsewhere, including Jesus' well-known parable of the "Good Samaritan." Based on what Jesus says in Matthew, I am certain to be rewarded with eternal life. I have two children, so I've been feeding the hungry, clothing the naked, and taking care of the sick for many years. And depending on how my son turns out, I may have the opportunity to visit him in prison.

Why, then, are there biblical passages such as John 14:6, where Jesus declares, "I am the way and the truth and the life. No one comes to the Father except through me" or John 6:53-57, which makes the following claim:

> So Jesus said to them, 'Very truly, I tell you, unless you eat the flesh of the Son of Man and drink his blood, you have no life in you. Those who eat my flesh and drink my blood have eternal life, and I will raise them up on the last day; for my flesh is true food and my blood is true drink...so whoever eats me will live because of me.

Such passages in John indicate a dispute among early Christians, with different sides insisting their view was the only correct one. Some Christians believed that Christ had come in the flesh, while others refused to accept this. They believed instead that the appearance of Christ was purely spiritual, since flesh was the product of sin. Simply put, the community that produced John's Gospel wrote these passages as invectives to criticize a rival Christian group who had a different view of Jesus. They were not intended for use as weapons to be wielded by the followers of one world religion against followers of a completely different one. Indeed, the disagreement over eating Jesus' flesh and drinking his blood continues today among the different Christian groups. Catholics and Orthodox Christians believe Christ is actually present in the bread and wine; while many Protestant Christians believe the presence of Jesus is strictly symbolic. I wonder which Christian group the Gospel of John's community would have rejected?

Every religion at various times has claimed superiority over another, especially when competing for followers and support in the same geographical area. More frequently, followers within the same religion competed with each other over interpretation of their teachings. This is behind the Theravada—Mahayana divide in Buddhism; the Sunni—Shia split in Islam; and the various schisms in Christianity.

The John writings reflect a conflict among believers in the same religion. Sometimes the dispute became acrimonious and splinter groups formed within the early Christian community as a result. This is made clear in 1 John 2:19:

> *They went out from us, but they did not belong to us; for if they had belonged to us they would have remained with us. But by going out they made it plain that none of them belongs to us.*

This passage does not refer to those in Buddhism, Judaism, Islam, Hinduism, or in any other religion. It is targeting a dissident Christian group. Those who lack a historical understanding of their own religious tradition, however, are liable to take scriptural passages out of context. Taking things out of context changes meanings. This explains in part how those who belong to the Christian tradition, which has such beauty to it, can say things so ugly and hateful to those who don't.

The Beloved Disciple

The previous article excited many readers. I received heartfelt thanks from those who experienced things similar to the student I wrote about, and defamatory messages from readers who identified with that student's friends.

Readers on both sides asked me to elaborate on the different views of Jesus reflected in John's Gospel and Matthew's Gospel. A detailed explanation would go beyond the limits of this article, however, so I'll keep things short and simple. For those wishing to study the issue further in an objective, scholarly manner, classes on the Bible are offered throughout the UH system, including at the campuses where I teach.

Different Christian groups had different ideas of who Jesus was and what it meant to be a follower of Christ. This was the case in first century Christianity and it is certainly true today. In his letters to the various Christian churches, for example, the Apostle Paul chastised members for creating divisions that threatened the Christian community. Rival factions had formed within the church based on allegiance to a particular apostle or church leader. This continues today as the Catholic Church claims to descend from the apostle Peter—who is regarded as the first pope—while the Orthodox Church claims apostolic succession from Andrew, another of Jesus' disciples. Protestant churches too, are tied to particular leaders and reject the teachings of the other two forms of Christianity. Do the gospels themselves favor a particular disciple over the others, thereby reflecting some of the cliques, factions, and rivalries?

Peter is perhaps the most prominent of Jesus' 12 disciples. Indeed, the Gospel of Matthew affords Peter special recognition. Only in Matthew's Gospel does Jesus give Peter the keys of heaven and proclaims that he will build his church specifically on Peter (Matthew 16).

The Gospel of John advocates a different disciple, however, a peculiar figure known as the "beloved disciple" (John 13:23), who only appears in

98

John's Gospel. What is more, John's Gospel makes it clear that this anonymous disciple had a stronger rapport with Jesus and was more intimate with him than any other disciple, including Peter.

For example, at the last meal Jesus has with his followers, the beloved disciple is seated closest to Jesus. In fact, the beloved disciple is leaning on Jesus' chest. He is so intimate with Jesus that Peter has to ask a question to Jesus through the beloved disciple. The implication here is that Peter (who may represent a different Christian group) must go through the beloved disciple (the Christian group that produced John's Gospel) to reach Jesus.

Secondly, whereas Peter denies Jesus three times after Jesus is arrested, the beloved disciple stays by Jesus' side during his interrogation by the high priest.

A third example occurs at the crucifixion scene. In Matthew's Gospel, none of Jesus' 12 disciples are present at Jesus' crucifixion. In John's Gospel, however, the beloved disciple is there with Jesus. The suggestion here is that unlike the other male disciples, Jesus' beloved disciple did not abandon Jesus during his suffering and death.

A fourth example occurs at the resurrection. Mary Magdalene finds the tomb of Jesus empty and runs to tell Peter and the beloved disciple about her discovery. The two disciples race to the tomb, but "the other disciple outran Peter and reached the tomb first." (John 20:4) The beloved disciple is the first to believe in the risen Christ. John's Gospel presents a literal race between Peter and the beloved disciple and the beloved disciple wins the competition.

A final example occurs at the reappearance of the resurrected Jesus. The disciples are fishing, but have no luck catching anything. The resurrected Jesus is standing on the shore but the disciples do not recognize him. After Jesus gives the disciples a fishing tip that results in a great catch, however, the disciple whom Jesus loved then realizes who it is and identifies Jesus to Peter. Peter did not know it was Jesus until told so by the beloved disciple.

Different gospels put forth different messianic traditions. In Matthew's Gospel, in order to fulfill messianic expectations, Jesus was: born of a virgin, baptized, tempted by Satan, someone who only taught in parables, in agony before his arrest, unaware of what the Father knows, and seemingly forsaken by God and his disciples at the cross. None of these events are in John's Gospel. Why not? In John's Gospel, Jesus is God in the flesh thus it makes little sense for God to experience any of the above. Which tradition is the right one?

According to John's Gospel, the beloved disciple was faithful and committed to Christ throughout, unlike the other disciples who abandoned, betrayed, or denied Jesus. The Gospel of John argues, therefore, that its view of Jesus is superior to other accounts because it is based on the narrative of Jesus' closest follower—the beloved disciple. And Christians can trust the account provided by the beloved disciple because "we know that his testimony is true." (John 21:24) This is behind the Gospel of John's attack on those who did not accept its views.

The different gospels reflect different apostolic and messianic traditions. Any introductory college textbook on the Bible will make this clear. And though John's Gospel called all Christians to love, some Christians condemned others for holding different views of Jesus. This continues today, as some of the emails I receive make clear.

The Real Reason
For The Season

Jesus is not the reason for the season. If anything, it's just the opposite. The same holds true with the other religious holidays celebrated in December. No one knows what time of the year Jesus was born. A Jewish tradition states that the messiah would be born on the 9th day of the Hebrew month of Av (July/August)—the date when the 1st and 2nd temples in Jerusalem were destroyed—so perhaps Jesus was born then. Complicating matters further, the four Christian gospels provide inconsistent details regarding the birth of Jesus: Was it Nazareth (Mark, John) or Bethlehem (Matthew, Luke)? In a house (Matthew) or manger (Luke)? Wise men (Matthew) or shepherds (Luke)? Infanticide (Matthew) or census (Luke)? Star (Matthew) or angel (Luke)?

The birth of Jesus was not much of a concern in the earliest Christian writings, for example in Paul's letters or Mark's Gospel. In fact, the first mention of a celebration of the birth of Christ did not occur until 200 years after Jesus died. Simply put, the birth of Jesus did not matter; the crucifixion of Christ did. If there is no biblical document telling us the time of the year when Jesus was born, how did December 25 get chosen? There are two possible theories.

Tertullian—one of the early Christian apologists who lived in the 3rd century and is probably best known for his association with the trinity concept—calculated the date of the crucifixion of Christ as March 25, based on John's Gospel (the other gospels have Jesus dying on a different day). In a number of religions there is the notion that salvation encompasses a cycle that connects the end with the beginning e.g. death and birth, destruction and creation. Theravada Buddhists, for example, believe the Buddha was born, achieved enlightenment, and died on the same day (albeit in different years). As already mentioned, a Jewish tradition ties the destruction of the Jerusalem temple with the birth of the messiah. The salvation cycle was present in Christianity, too. Christians believed the crucifixion and conception of Christ occurred on the same day, March 25. This explains why in the Christian calendar, March 25 celebrates Annunciation, when the angel Gabriel announced to Mary that she would give birth to Christ. December 25 and Christmas are simply nine months after March 25 and Annunciation.

A more popular theory takes into account Christianity's penchant for incorporating non-Christian practices into its own. Winter solstice marks the longest night of the year in the northern hemisphere and occurs in late December. For those in antiquity, the days leading up to winter solstice may have seemed to be a time when the forces of death and darkness threatened and could possibly overcome the powers of light and life. Certain symbols therefore—evergreen tree, candles—were utilized in various cultures as hopeful expressions of the power of light in its struggle against darkness. After winter solstice, darkness gradually begins to give way to light as the sun reasserts itself and the length of the day increases. The birth of the sun god was therefore associated with this time of the year and celebrated in Rome on December 25. This idea appealed to Christians celebrating the birth of God's son, the light of the world. Thus the birth of the sun god became the birth of God's son. In other words, Christians incorporated a non-Christian festival into its faith. This explains why a small number of Christian groups do not celebrate Christmas: it was originally a pagan holiday.

There are universal themes in religion that do not belong solely to one group or another, but are shared across different traditions and by different people. The celebration of light over darkness during this time of the year is one such theme. Bodhi Day (Enlightenment Day) in Buddhism and Hanukkah (Festival of Lights) in Judaism are expressions of this. Christmas is too.

December is also the time of the year when we think about giving and receiving gifts. We are thankful for the presents from others, and for the presence of others. They light up our lives. And yet our lives are not only ours, but made up of the lives of others. All of us have special ones who have loved us unconditionally—through countless sacrifices, acts of kindness, patience, and caring—and they have helped us become who we are. Some are here, some are far away, and some may no longer be in this world. Some may be sitting right next to you as you read this. They are the ones who care about us and want what is best for us in life. They may not have a holiday dedicated to them, but they light up our lives just the same. And let us hope that we've added some light to theirs. This, to me, is the real reason for the season. And as the favorite child of my parents, I know I light up their lives. In fact, I'm so bright my dad calls me, "son."

Fake News;
Real Consequences

Fake news is seemingly everywhere nowadays. But fake news is not something new—it has been around for centuries. In fact, some might argue that religion is the result of fake news. Reports of a man being taken up to heaven on a winged horse, another man battling demons while sitting under a tree before achieving enlightenment, or more than two million slaves miraculously escaping through a parted sea and given laws on a mountain from a voice in a burning bush—are all incredible stories that are not verified by independent sources. They are propagated even today to sway the views of people. Fake news. Or so it seems.

The resurrection of Jesus is another fantastic story.

The three-day period from Good Friday to Easter Sunday is the most sacred time in Christianity. Good Friday commemorates the crucifixion of Jesus, while Easter Sunday celebrates his resurrection. To those outside the Christian tradition, it may seem odd to label the day that marks the suffering and humiliating death of Jesus as "good." Why is it good that Jesus was tortured and crucified? Christians believe that his death was a sacrifice for the sins of the world.

Christians also believe that God raised Jesus from the dead. And since death is the product of sin, Christians believe that not only does Jesus have power over death—if he didn't, he'd still be dead—but over sin as well. In short, Christians believe that Jesus died for our sins and was raised for our justification—so that we may be made right with God. This is the central belief in Christianity and expressed in a number of ways, including in the practice of baptism—where we ritually die to our old selves and a new self is raised.

This seemingly straightforward Christian view of the death and resurrection of Christ gets complicated when presented to students in a world religions class that is a mixture of those who are firm believers in their faith, those on the lookout for fake news, and those who don't care one way or the other.

Some wonder why God couldn't come up with a better plan than one that demanded the torture and death of his only son? He is God, after all. Other options must have been available. What is more, it is completely baffling to non-believers why people should praise and celebrate this plan of violence by a father for his innocent son. If a father demanded the torture and death of his child in our society, we'd have him arrested.

My task as a religion teacher is to present the religious traditions to students in a manner that is fair to the respective religions and their followers, but does not gloss over the shortcomings of the various faiths either. My goal is to simply help students make sense out of the non-sense. The resurrection of Christ is a challenge in this regard.

To skeptics who doubt that the resurrection actually happened and consider the whole Christian account as fake news, I ask them to see the story as a myth—a symbolic story that may or may not be historically true, but can convey a profound truth. In this way, the story is meaningful, even for non-believers.

Easter Sunday occurs in the spring, when flora and fauna resurrect from the ground after a winter of hibernation. We too, can reemerge after periods of darkness.

We are the products of relationships and experiences, some of which have had a profound impact on our lives. The loss of a loved one, for example, changes us. A part of us dies too, and we reemerge as a different person—one with a deeper understanding and a greater appreciation for the person lost and the relationship shared. This change doesn't only occur with physical death, but whenever there is a significant loss—a job, a home, or one's youth, for example.

Resurrection, then, is not limited to the gods, but something we can do for others. We can revive each other—by offering a helping hand or a kind word—and give the vulnerable new life. This is a message expressed in religions but transcends them as well.

To those who would reject such a figurative interpretation of Christ's resurrection in favor of a more literal and traditional understanding, I would point out that there are real implications for living in this world from this perspective as well.

Since Jesus rose bodily, the flesh must be important. This in turn means the body is valued. We are charged, then, to care for our bodies—to feed the hungry, take care of the sick, and welcome the lost by making sure that everyone has healthcare and shelter so that they too may have life. Those who believe in a literal interpretation of the resurrection but do not care for bodies—theirs and others—reject its basic message. What, then, does belief in a literal resurrection mean for such people? Not much.

Religions may be fake news, but they give us real consequences.

Jesus The Messiah

Jesus is the messiah. At least he is according to the Quran. In this regard the Quran and the Christian Bible concur. However, while Muslims and Christians agree that Jesus is the messiah, they do not agree on the details of his crucifixion or indeed whether Jesus was crucified at all.

In Christianity, the date of Jesus' crucifixion was important to note because Christians believed Jesus died on the same day that he was conceived (albeit in different years). In turn, the date of Jesus' conception and crucifixion became key for calculating Jesus' birth, which would occur nine months later. The Christian Church believed that Jesus was conceived and crucified on March 25 (Annunciation).

Muslims do not.

According to Surah 4:157-158 in the Quran, Jesus wasn't crucified. Someone else who looked like Jesus was instead. Imagine the luck of that guy. Most Christians would find this view of Jesus bizarre, for the Gospels clearly state that Jesus was hung on the cross.

Muslims, however, believe that while the Gospels were initially from God, they were subsequently corrupted. In the view of Islam, not only do the Gospels mistakenly believe Jesus was crucified, but the Gospels wrongfully command their readers to worship him too. In Surah 5:116-117, Jesus corrects this misunderstanding and denies ever teaching his followers that they should worship him. Jesus proclaims that Allah alone is to be worshipped instead. Muslims believe only the Quran is perfect, while Christians believe in the Gospel truth.

Whether or not the Gospels or the Quran is true is besides the point here. Of greater interest to scholars are the varying and fascinating beliefs and stories about Jesus that the scriptural traditions reflect.

Students find it amusing that several places in the world claim to have the grave of Jesus, including Japan. Christ's grave is in Aomori prefecture in northeastern Japan. According to the information plaque at the gravesite, Jesus came to Japan at age 21 to study theology and returned to Judea when he was 33. But his teachings were rejected and the Roman authorities attempted to crucify him. However, Jesus' brother was crucified instead and Jesus returned to Japan, raised a family, and lived until 106 years old. According to this strange Japanese tale, Jesus was not crucified. Someone who resembled him—his brother—was instead. Did early Christians believe Jesus had a brother who could have been mistaken for him?

There were several books that did not make it into the Christian Bible. Although the Christian churches ultimately rejected these books, these non-canonical writings provide insight into the variety of ways early Christians understood who Jesus was. The Infancy Gospel of Thomas, for example, tells of what Jesus was like as a child. According to the author, boy Jesus had a mischievous streak and a hot temper and sometimes misused his supernatural powers to satisfy both (at the expense of unsuspecting victims). The author of this gospel claims to be Thomas. What is interesting here is that the name Thomas literally means "twin." Whose twin? Jesus' twin. And who would know Jesus' childhood better than his own twin? Some early Christians believed Jesus had a twin, Thomas. This claim may seem odd to most Christians today, but there are several other non-canonical writings that profess to be based on Thomas, including the Acts of Thomas, which makes it explicitly clear that Thomas was Jesus' twin.

What about the Christian Bible, what do the books there tell us about the crucifixion? The first three gospels in the New Testament—Matthew, Mark, and Luke—tell the story of the Roman soldiers who, after flogging Jesus and spitting on him, forced a man named Simon of Cyrene to carry Jesus' cross to the place of execution. Interestingly, the scene concerning Simon is not in the last gospel, the Gospel of John. Why not? There are several possible reasons, including the notion that not only did Simon carry the cross for Jesus, but that he was ultimately crucified for him as well.

This is made clear in The Second Treatise of the Great Seth, a 3rd century Gnostic Christian writing that denies the crucifixion of Jesus. According to this text, Christ transformed Simon of Cyrene into his own likeness; and Simon was thus crucified in place of Jesus. This of course is rejected in orthodox Christianity. The writer(s) of John's Gospel was probably aware of the teachings of Gnostic Christians, and perhaps to remove any doubt that Jesus was crucified, deleted the Simon episode altogether from the last gospel.

A messiah crucified for others? Someone else crucified for the messiah? A messiah not crucified at all? This month many of us will celebrate the humble birth of a man who gave birth to fascinating traditions regarding the messiah.

What Is So Traditional About Marriage?

It's odd that there are still some people who oppose same-sex marriage under the pretense of preserving traditional marriage. I oppose traditional marriage. I suspect too, that those who publicly claim to support traditional marriage really don't, at least not on biblical grounds. After all, exactly which form of biblical marriage should be held up as the traditional model? Polygamy? The great biblical figures had multiple wives. Indeed Solomon, to whom God gave wisdom and insight, had 700 wives. If not polygamy, then what about other forms of traditional marriage found in books of the Bible such as Deuteronomy, Ezra, Nehemiah, and elsewhere, which forbid inter-racial marriage? Because of this Bible-based form of traditional marriage, it was illegal in parts of the United States up until 1967 to marry outside of one's ethnicity. My one wife and I come from different ethnic, cultural, and religious backgrounds, and our relationship is enriched as a result. I am sure there are many others in Hawai'i in racially mixed relationships who feel similarly. Yet such relationships would be in violation of traditional marriage, according to certain books in the Bible, and our relationships would be considered criminal and viewed as immoral had not such discriminatory laws been changed in the United States.

In the biblical tradition, a woman did not have the right to divorce her husband. (There are Christian churches today that view divorce as sin, citing passages from Mark and Malachi for support.) Because of this form of traditional marriage where women enjoyed few rights, it was not acceptable in the United States for a woman to vote, hold elective office, attend college, or divorce an abusive husband. Indeed, before the Equal Credit Opportunity Act in 1974, a woman had difficulty obtaining a loan or a credit card on her own.

Even more astonishing, marital rape was only recognized as a criminal act by all 50 states in 1993. Before this, a husband could not be found guilty of non-consensual sex with his wife. Biblical passages such as 1 Corinthians 7, which states that a married person does not have authority over one's own body, but the spouse does instead, played a role in the ethos that shaped this form of traditional marriage where a husband could not be found guilty of raping his wife.

There are still other forms of traditional marriage I do not support. For example the traditional marriage where the wife is not allowed to have a career, but must stay home while the husband works as the sole provider. Wives (and husbands) who choose to work in the home deserve respect. However, careers can be just as fulfilling and life transforming, and in our times who would oppose the idea of a woman having the opportunity to gain an education so that she might pursue her own professional goals?

Some believe the arrival of Jesus Christ freed one from being bound to all the laws of the Bible, as Christ heralded a new tradition. In other words traditions changed, the old gave way to the new, the traditional was no longer tradition. According to many in the Christian faith, Jesus was not married. The traditional form of marriage thus became no marriage. This explains the rise and development of monks and nuns in Christianity, as they sought to emulate Jesus' celibate life. If Christians are those who aspire to be Christ-like, married Christians continue to fail in this regard.

Beliefs about traditional marriage extend to notions of traditional family as well, where ideas and shapes of the family have evolved. Single or divorced parents along with their biological or adopted children and their children's step-siblings and half siblings are all family, despite being outside the traditional model.

The above issues center on the definition of tradition, but the real problem lies not in the definition of tradition, but in the misunderstanding of its function. Traditions are meant to provide continuity, not constraint. They inspire and stir innovation, and should not be invoked to mask discrimination. For many, knowledge and appreciation of one's own tradition serve as a wellspring for personal growth. In short, tradition is the source of change. In this regard traditions are more akin to bridges and pathways rather than fences and gates. Standing tradition is thus an oxymoron.

It is an indisputable fact that the concepts and forms of marriage have changed over time. Change is thus a tradition of marriage. Those who seek to confine marriage to its traditional forms, therefore, violate the tradition of marriage.

ON ISLAM

A Religion Of Peace?

Words with the Semitic tri-consonantal root "slm" are often associated with peace and well-being. The Hebrew word that people use to greet others with—*shalom*—is a good example. The Arabic equivalent is *salaam*. The tri-consonantal root "slm" is also at the core of a religion called, Islam.

Some insist that Islam is a religion of peace. Others find it ironic that a religion that has "peace" at the heart of its name is associated with violence. I don't. The basic message at the center of all the major world religions is peace; yet followers of every religion have at one time or another committed acts of violence and atrocities for the sake of this message and in the name of their faith. Not many people in America associate Buddhism with violence, for example, but many victims of religiously-backed hatred in Sri Lanka, Thailand, and Myanmar do. There, some Buddhist monks engage in discriminatory rhetoric to incite violence against ethnic and religious minorities. Yet the majority of Buddhists are peaceful and compassionate. The same can be said about Muslims.

It is thus a distortion to label a particular religion as inherently violent. It is also inaccurate to claim that the same religion is fundamentally peaceful. It is both and neither. What novelist Chimamanda Ngozi Adichie says about the dangers of stereotypes and a single story can be applied to religion: Reducing a religion or a people to a single narrative produces an incomplete and potentially dangerous understanding of a faith and its believers. Labels and stereotypes may be convenient, but they mask richness and complexity. Thus the stereotype of Islam as a violent religion is not untrue, but it is not complete either. (Likewise, the stereotype of a religion professor and columnist as good-looking is not false—but it's not all that I am.)

There are violent and peaceful followers in every religion because there are violent and peaceful people everywhere. In fact, the potential for violence and peace exists within the same person. Religion happens to be an effective means to express both tendencies.

Many who are not very familiar with Islam are aware of a few, if misconstrued, Muslim concepts. Perhaps the best case in point is the notion of *jihad*. Jihad is often translated as *holy war*. While jihad can mean war, its literal meaning is *striving* or *effort*. The Arabic word for war, on the other hand, is *harb*.

After returning from battle, the prophet Muhammad is purported to have said that there are two kinds of jihad. One type of jihad encourages Muslims to battle against the weaknesses in society or dangers that threaten society—which can mean fighting injustice and oppression, and spreading and defending Islam, if necessary, through armed struggle or holy war. The other kind of jihad (known as the greater jihad) requires Muslims to struggle against the weaknesses within the self—to be virtuous and moral, making a serious effort to do good works and help to reform society.

While the term *jihad* is distinctively tied to Islam, the concept of jihad is not. Other religions also have notions of waging a battle against one's own shortcomings while demanding that its followers work towards creating a just and peaceful society. There is both the call to battle and the desire for peace. To insist a religion is intrinsically characterized by only one side is to neglect the diversity and complexity of the religious tradition and creates division in the religion instead.

Diversity is a good thing, division less so. The threat to religion is the former can easily slide into the latter. Peace and violence exist in Islam—one the product of accepting diversity; the other a likely consequence of division.

Islam may be called violent in one context; and peaceful in another. These labels are shaped by various conditions that amplify some voices and curtail others. Therefore, when we hear assertions about Islam or any other religion—both positive and negative—we have to consider the speaker and the source of the voice. Is it a voice speaking from diversity or division?

Who speaks for Islam? More importantly, whose voice do we listen to when defining Islam? And most important of all—why do we choose to listen to that particular voice and not others? Peace or violence; diversity or division. One can hear what one wants to in any religion.

Ramadan

If variety is the spice of life, religion is its dessert. Indulged in the right amount and enjoyed with others at the appropriate time, religion can be a nice complement to an already fulfilling life. Feasting on it as if it were the sole offering on a buffet line, however, or using it for unrestrained, self-gratification harms the spirit and body. Too much dessert is not good. Indeed, "desserts" spelled backwards is "stressed."

The lifestyle and practices of those different from us become intolerable and distasteful when we overindulge in our own faith. Fortunately, religions have built in practices that restore the balance between the pursuit of salvation or enlightenment for one's own sake, and compassion and forgiveness for the sake of others. Fasting is one such practice.

There are good reasons to fast, including health benefits. The body is good at cleansing itself of unhealthy substances. The liver, lungs, colon, kidneys, lymph glands, and even our skin get rid of impurities. However, the body has trouble ridding itself of toxins when it is consistently fed poor food. Fasting helps the body remove the buildup of waste products in our bodies.

For people of faith, fasting not only cleanses the body, but rejuvenates the spirit as well. One of the best-known religious fasts is Ramadan.

Ramadan is a sacred month in Islam. Many significant events occurred during this month in the history of Islam, but none more important than the first revelation from God through the angel Gabriel to Muhammad, whom Muslims believe was the last and greatest of all the prophets. Ramadan is the month that revealed the Quran.

Ramadan is actually the name of the 9th month in the Muslim calendar, and because Muslims follow a lunar calendar, Ramadan arrives roughly 11 days earlier each year (solar year = 365 ¼ days; lunar year = 354 days). This means Ramadan moves through the seasons and can occur in the winter, fall, summer, or spring.

During Ramadan, Muslims are not allowed to eat anything, drink anything, smoke anything, fight anything, or have sex with anything for the entire month—during daylight hours. This can be particularly trying when Ramadan falls in the summer months and the days are long. Not all Muslims, however, are required to observe Ramadan with a fast. The young, the elderly, the sick, pregnant women, and women who have their menses are exempt. A Muslim friend jokingly said, "It's basically just men, then."

Complete abstinence from sunrise to sunset is difficult. Yet at a time when Muslims may feel most weak and vulnerable, knowing that millions of other Muslims are fasting at the same time provides a strong sense of community to rely on for support and encouragement.

Fasting requires self-discipline. During Ramadan Muslims are to purify their spirit, reflect on their shortcomings, and resist the tendency to speak ill of others, gossip, or argue. Controlling the self also fosters compassion for others, as Ramadan provides Muslims with a yearly glimpse of how those less fortunate in the world live and feel. As a result, Muslims not only deny themselves during Ramadan, but give of themselves in the form of charity to the poor. The body may be denied food, but the spirit is nourished.

At the conclusion of Ramadan, Muslims gather with friends and family to celebrate a three-day festival known as Eid al-Fitr (Festival of Breaking the Fast), where special prayers are offered and food and gifts are exchanged.

For the poor and less fortunate of all faiths in different parts of the world, however, a fast continues, albeit an involuntarily one. For these people they do what they can to live, whether socially acceptable or not, whether sanctioned by their faith or not.

Ideally, fasting promotes self-control and compassion for others. In contrast, when one indulges in religion to such an extent that one is full of one's own faith, it becomes easy to dismiss the downtrodden and those who follow a different path. Ironically, those who gorge on such religious fare end up consumed by their religious beliefs. For these, a fast from their faith might be a good idea.

ON HINDUISM

Holy Cow

Holy Cow! Jesus was not always God (though the Gospel of John claims this), the Buddha was not always eternal (though the Lotus Sutra claims this), and the Quran was…always the Quran (just as it is stated in the Quran). But the cow was not always sacred in Hinduism (though Hindu nationalists insist this was so).

Religions and cultures tend to romanticize the past (and idealize a distant future), claiming their beliefs and practices descend from sacred origins or enlightened ancestors. This tendency is especially appealing to those of us who are dissatisfied with contemporary society or who view the challenges of modernity as overly stressful and empty of meaning.

In response, we recreate the past as a way to construct our identity in the present. We re-imagine a way of life that never was. We then claim it as a treasured tradition that must be defended from threats of change, including the introduction of foreign ideas, practices, and people. Cow veneration and the rejection of beef-eating in Hinduism are examples of this.

India is roughly 80% Hindu and the cow enjoys venerated status in contemporary society. One can see cows wandering the streets in India bringing traffic to a halt. They are not harmed. What is more, because of the cow's standing in Hinduism, eating beef is met with disdain and even banned in numerous places. When I was in India a few years ago and suffered from a mild case of "Delhi belly," I sought comfort food at a McDonald's. I was surprised by what was (and wasn't) on the menu—no beef. Even at Indian eateries here in Hawai'i one will not find beef on the menu.

Cow veneration and the accompanying prohibition on beef-eating have thus become hallmarks of Hindu identity. They are also rallying symbols wielded by many Hindus against non-Hindu traditions.

There are calls for a nationwide ban on killing cows (currently 20 out of 36 states and territories in India forbid the slaughter of cows). Indeed, in some places in India it is illegal to even hold a hamburger, and eating beef could cost the offender $150 in fines and up to five years in prison.

But the notion of the cow as a sacred animal did not always exist in the earliest forms of Hinduism. In fact, there are no cow goddesses or temples to cows even in contemporary Hinduism. Scholarly evidence is clear that the cow was not considered sacred when the oldest scriptures in Hinduism—the Vedas—were produced. Instead, there are references to cows sacrificed and eaten. As India shifted to an agrarian based economy, however, certain animals—including cows—became valuable for small-scale farming. From this, special status was accorded to the cow. The concept of the "Holy Cow" was later created and employed to shape Hindu identity in its competition against two rival religious and cultural practices.

Buddhism began in India. As the religion developed and gained influence, it criticized the beliefs and practices of other religious traditions, including elaborate rituals involved in sacrificing cows. As a counter to the Buddhist critique, a form of Hinduism arose that banned the killing of cows and beef-eating altogether. Vegetarianism later emerged as an ideal in certain forms of Hinduism and this allowed the religion to claim superiority over Buddhism, since Buddhist monks were not vegetarians (indeed, the Buddha himself ate meat).

Food can also be politicized and utilized as a weapon to foment prejudice and cast aspersions on an entire religion. Muslims eat beef. In India, Hindu nationalists use their diet as a means to distinguish themselves from the nation's beef-eating (and implicitly immoral) Muslim minority. The current attempt to criminalize cow slaughter and beef-eating nationwide in India may be viewed from the conflict between Hindu identity and Islam. Muslims predominantly run the beef industry in India, thus there have been calls for beef-eaters to leave India and move to neighboring Pakistan (where Islam is the state religion). Religious and cultural fundamentalists have fabricated and promoted the myth that Muslims introduced beef eating and a host of other ills to India. But xenophobia is not unique to India and Hindu culture.

There are those in every religion and culture who insist there is only one truth or one way of life. In India, Hindu nationalists claim there is one unchanging and eternal Hinduism, which just so happens to be their own. Are there equivalents in our state? What sacred cows do we create and hold up as revered traditions to define and distinguish ourselves from others? What sacred cows do we invoke to halt change, impede progress and divide people? For some it is a divine man, for others a holy book, and for still others it is a sacred mountain. And that's no bull.

ON SHINTO

Shinto Values

Shinto is the native religion of Japan and there are five Shinto shrines on O'ahu—Izumo Taishakyo Mission of Hawai'i (Downtown), Ishizuchi Jinja (Mō'ili'ili), Daijingu Temple of Hawai'i (Nu'uanu), Wakamiya Inari Shrine (Waipahu), and Hawai'i Kotohira Jinsha–Hawai'i Dazaifu Tenmangu (Kalihi). The shrines offer visitors respite from the bustling activity of everyday life in the world around us; and from the stresses and complications of thoughts and emotions in the world within. To most people, however, it is not readily apparent what the official teachings of Shinto are. To be sure, one would be hard-pressed to identify explicit doctrines or creeds the equivalent of the iconic teachings found in other world religions such as the Ten Commandments (Judaism), Holy Trinity (Christianity), Five Pillars of Faith (Islam), or Four Noble Truths (Buddhism).

Instead of dogmas or specific articles of faith, there are overarching values and underlying themes that permeate Shinto traditions and perspectives. Visit any Shinto shrine and one will notice an emphasis on purity, nature, simplicity and gratitude.

Purity

Purity is perhaps the most prominent value emphasized in Shinto. Indeed, the first thing visitors see when approaching a Shinto shrine is the torii, a tall gateway structure consisting of two pillars and two crossbeams. The torii separates the realm of purity from the world of pollution; but also functions as a passageway from one side to the other. The torii usually marks the official entrance to a Shinto shrine, though sometimes a torii may stand unattached to any religious place of worship.

The largest torii on the island, for example, stands alone and seemingly out of place in Mōʻiliʻili Triangle Park. Yet on one side of the 25 foot vermillion structure is an all-natural health food store; while on the other side is a fast-food place. Thus even though there is no Shinto shrine present in the immediate vicinity, the Mōʻiliʻili torii still fulfills its symbolic function of contrasting and connecting separate realms.

After passing through the torii at a Shinto shrine, however, the emphasis on purity continues, as it is customary for visitors to pause at a water basin to cleanse themselves by washing their hands and rinsing their mouths before proceeding to offer prayers to the gods. A Shinto priest may then wave a wand consisting simply of white paper streamers over the bowed heads of the shrine visitors for blessing and purification. As a further expression of purity, footwear must be removed when entering the sanctuary or main hall of a Shinto shrine.

One may also notice the presence of straw ropes (shimenawa) hanging from various places in the shrine precinct. They mark the presence of the sacred. Fans of sumo know that grand champions (yokozuna) also wear a straw rope belt around their waists, a symbol of their revered status.

Nature

Straw ropes may also be found outside of the shrine compound tied to, from, or around various things in nature such as rocks, mountains, waterfalls and trees—all of which may be viewed as abodes of the sacred in Shinto.

The offerings placed at the altar in the shrine reflect the importance of the natural world too, as it is common to present things from nature to the gods. For example, branch clippings from the Japanese evergreen tree (sakaki) are commonly used as offerings and for purification blessings.

Also, Shinto shrines in Japan are often built without nails and left unpainted or painted in natural colors, another example of the Shinto appreciation for things in its natural state.

Simplicity

In contrast to Buddhist temples, where the sights, sounds, and smells of the temples can be bewildering and overwhelming, Shinto shrines are simple affairs. It is rare for visitors to a Shinto shrine to see elaborate images or statues and ritual implements that are commonly found at Buddhist temples. Shinto shrines exude a sense of things being plain, calm and simple. Shinto shrines convey clarity instead of clutter, decorum instead of decoration.

Gratitude

Japanese bow to show respect and appreciation. Thus when addressing the gods at a Shinto shrine, it is customary to bow several times (supplicants generally bow twice, clap their hands twice, and bow once more). The emphasis on gratitude is so ingrained in Japan that it is not uncommon to see people on cell phones bowing to the person they are having a conversation with. But like the god(s) that we bow down to, it's hard to know if the one on the other end is aware of our gesture.

That being said, the next time you stand before a torii—whether at a Shinto shrine or on the patch of land where King and Beretania streets meet in Mōʻiliʻili—take note of the world around you and of the world within you. Notice too, which side of the torii you are on and be thankful that the other side is only a few steps away.

Omamori

Omamori and ofuda are spiritual charms, talismans, and amulets in the Japanese religious tradition that possess the power to ward off misfortune and procure good luck. They can be made of pieces of wood, patches of cloth, strips of paper, or rings of metal and come in various sizes, though the majority found in Hawaiʻi tend to be no larger than the size of one's palm.

Whereas ofuda are usually placed in a home or business, attached to a wall or door entrance to provide spiritual protection for the entire site, omamori tend to be portable and can often be seen dangling from car rearview mirrors or pasted on the bumpers and windows of cars, where they are at once expressions of faith and portals of magical power. Omamori can also be worn on the body and like ofuda, are symbols of protection of the Buddhas and kami. It is even fashionable to attach omamori to handbags, schoolbags, and cellphones.

Omamori and ofuda are often inscribed with the name of a specific temple or shrine and the particular power or blessing charged to them. Hawaiʻi Kotohira Jinsha-Hawaiʻi Dazaifu Tenmangu is known for its wide selection of omamori and ofuda, many of which are unique to Hawaiʻi. However, omamori and ofuda that are commonly found at temples and shrines are dedicated to traffic safety, protection from natural disasters, good health, theft prevention and family blessing. Charms to ensure strong and lasting relationships and talismans to help one succeed in school or business are also popular. One may even purchase golf or Las Vegas omamori, to help ensure good luck for the wearer. Though omamori represent spiritual power and protection, believers say the benefits they provide are concrete, practical, and real.

Different shrines and temples may also have omamori unique to their teaching or practice. Members of Zaoji Temple in Kalihi, for instance, wear snake ring omamori on their fingers. The snake is a manifestation of water or mountain deities and just as the habitat of the snake crosses the borders between mountain and sea, so too the power of the snake kami is effective in diverse situations. Another interesting form of spiritual protection is found at Ishizuchi Shrine in Mōʻiliʻili. During certain rituals, the shrine offers its members paper dolls, which they are to place under their pillows to absorb all the negative energies in their lives. The paper dolls are subsequently burned in a sacred fire to get rid of the bad luck. Dolls purchased and displayed during Girls' Day may have once served a similar function in Japan.

Omamori represent the magical side to religion. If religion is slow magic, then omamori are quick religion. They provide short-cuts to happiness for the faithful by finding detours around moments of melancholy and anxiety.

I visit churches, temples, mosques, synagogues, and shrines on a regular basis and I find the gods and buddhas quite welcoming and unassuming. (It's their followers who are sometimes not too pleased with me.) On one occasion a few years ago, a woman at a Buddhist temple in Mōʻiliʻili smashed her car on her way to the temple's evening service. As I helped her from her wrecked car to make sure she was okay, several temple followers immediately pointed to the omamori decal pasted on her car and excitedly claimed that this is what had saved her from certain bodily injury. No one questioned why the omamori did not prevent the accident in the first place. Religion always works from the perspective of faith. What mattered most was that the woman suffered no serious physical harm when in other instances she would have. (Had the woman suffered bodily injury, followers would have probably pointed out that she did not die. Had she died, followers would have then claimed she died in the best way or is now in a better place.) Omamori, like faith, and like magic, always work.

Anyone can buy omamori. Indeed, the serious believer and the casual tourist alike purchase omamori at temples, shrines, and department stores. Omamori may function as symbols of salvation or as simply souvenirs, the one creating sacred experiences and the other preserving them.

Omamori create order and preserve meaning where happenstance and misfortune once were. In omamori the beliefs of followers meet the magic of religion.

Shichigosan

I was born again in the maternity ward at a local hospital a lifetime ago. When our baby girl came into the world a new father was born as well. I remember holding my daughter for the first time and wanting the moment to last a lifetime. I was reborn again four years later and lucky enough to have had the same experience with the birth of my son.

Every November over the course of several years, my wife and I took our daughter and son to a local Shinto shrine (Hawaiʻi Kotohira Jinsha –Hawaiʻi Dazaifu Tenmangu) for the Shichigosan (7-5-3) festival. Shichigosan is a time when children ages 7, 5, and 3 dress in special clothes—usually a kimono for girls and a hakama for boys—and are placed under the protective blessing of the kami (guardian deity). Shichigosan is an expression of a rite of passage, a ritual that marks the shifts and transitions from one social status to another. Age three marks the end of babyhood in Japanese custom, at five children begin to have formal relationships with other adults in the community outside of the family structure (school teachers, for example), and seven is a symbolic number in many religious traditions, signifying completion or fullness. At seven, then, a child has experienced the full richness of childhood and will soon prepare to enter the next stage of development, the so-called tween phase. The innocent years begin to give way to those that place a greater importance on the development, maturation and reliance on experience and critical thinking faculties instead. During Shichigosan, parents thank the kami for blessings received and ask for continued guidance and protection for their children so that their children may live full and healthy lives. For the children, more importantly, they receive special candies and treats symbolizing long life.

We visited the local Shinto shrines and participated in the Shichigosan festivities when our children were at the appropriate ages not simply because we wanted to enjoy a traditional religious rite, but more importantly because we believed in celebrating our children's childhood. One of the basic messages in Japanese religions is that everything is impermanent. Life is fleeting and hence it should be appreciated fully. The cherry blossom symbolizes this and explains in part why the cherry blossom is cherished in Japan: it appears in full bloom for a few weeks and then it is gone. The innocence and wonder of childhood is like this.

I don't remember how much longer after turning seven that I stopped holding my parents' hands, but I know that that was a step in the process of letting go and becoming my own person. Now, for the past several years my children have been engaged in something similar. And because our daughter is preparing to leave her parents' home and further the process of forging her own identity and finding her own path, I want to appreciate the last remnants of her childhood as much as I can before it is completely gone. She will always be my child and a wonderful playmate to the child that still hides in me, but soon she will have the grown-up responsibility of watching over this heart of mine that she will take with her wherever she goes. My son will not have that burden, as he tends to lose things.

So I will enjoy this time in my children's lives. This period when they are still with me—occasionally because they want to be with me and not just because they are obligated to or because I am forcing them to. This is still a time when they look to my wife and me for guidance—albeit with less frequency and with less uncritical acceptance of what we have to offer. I do miss the days when they used to hold our hands when walking, when they wanted us to carry them when they were tired, and when they kissed us goodnight after reading them bedtime stories. My wife and I now watch them with awe and pride at the young adults they are too quickly becoming. Truth be told, we still hold our children's hands, carry them when they are tired, and kiss them at the end of each day—though in slightly different ways from when they were little and in a manner in which they don't yet fully understand. And if we are fortunate enough to live long lives, a time will come when they will in turn do those things for us. The Shichigosan festival, then, is a celebration of childhood, an appreciation for the gift of parenthood, and an acknowledgment that one transitions into the other.

Yakudoshi

In various cultures there is widespread belief that there are certain crucial years in a person's life where one experiences important physical, mental, and/or social changes. In the Japanese religious tradition, these critical years are known as "yakudoshi."

Yakudoshi can be understood in part as an attempt to provide order and structure to our constantly changing lives. Yakudoshi signals an occasion when the different pieces of a person—body, mind, and spirit—are in near balance, whereas at other periods in a person's life one part is dominant over the others. Thus yakudoshi marks a critical stage in adulthood where the opportunity for a person to fully realize his or her potential in life is most available.

There is confusion among some families in Hawai'i, however, as to exactly when yakudoshi should be observed. For example, some maintain yakudoshi occurs when a man turns 41 years old, while others claim it is not until he's 42. This confusion stems in part from Japan's change to a western-based calendar system in the late 19th century, a period when the first Japanese immigrants began to make their way to Hawai'i. Before this, Japan based its calendar on the Chinese model. According to the old Japanese calendar, a baby was considered one year old at birth. (This makes sense, as a 40 week old baby at birth is closer to 12 months than 0 months.) After adopting the new western-based calendar, however, a baby was not considered a year old until one year after its birth. Thus in former times a 41-year old man in America was counted as 42 in Japan.

Why 42 and what is so special about this age? The power of yakudoshi resides in part in the homonymic qualities of the numbers involved. Pronouncing the numbers 4 (shi) and 2 (ni) in Japanese sounds like the Japanese word for death (shini). 42 is thus an age of crisis as it signals the end of a particular stage in a man's life. The Japanese word for crisis (kiki) is written with two Chinese characters, one meaning "danger" and the other meaning "opportunity." This suggests that in every crisis there exists the potential for danger and opportunity. The notion behind a man's yakudoshi, then, is that at 42 a man is at a critical juncture in life as his combined social, physical, and mental powers are near their peak. In short, at 42 a man should be making his mark in society. After this, his opportunities to do so dwindle.

Women have yakudoshi too, but the critical age is 33, not 42. Like the males' yakudoshi, there is a homonymic quality to the number. Pronouncing the numbers 3 (san) and 3 (zan) together sounds like the Japanese word for misery (sanzan). In other words, a woman is in full bloom at this age and will not be happy if she is not making the most of her potential during this period. In the past, this usually meant she should be married with children by this age otherwise her chances to experience these meaningful events will be lost. Luckily, most of us no longer live in the past.

It is customary to visit a shrine and receive the blessings of the gods during one's yakudoshi. This is done in the hopes that the critical year will be filled with good fortune and danger avoided. It is also common in Hawai'i for family and friends to throw yakudoshi parties to celebrate the birthday person's status, to ensure that this important year gets off to a good start, and to ask that the year brings more opportunities than dangers.

It is said we are not born all at once, but by bits. Our bodies are born first, and our spirit and character later. In the Japanese tradition of yakudoshi is both the opportunity to unite the disparate parts of a person's life, and the danger of letting them fall to pieces. May the gods, families and friends of those celebrating yakudoshi help keep the person together as long as possible. My own yakudoshi was a while ago and I've been falling apart ever since.

Eating Yourself

Our identity is tied to food. We define ourselves in part by the foods we eat (and don't eat). Our diet in turn is a conduit to cultural and religious values as the offerings at local gravesites and ritual foods used in worship and holidays make clear e.g. vegetarian jai for Buddhists celebrating Chinese New Year, sacrificed meat for Muslims celebrating Eid al-Adha.

Food is defined not only by its ingredients, but also by wider notions of purity and pollution, delicacy and disgust, that are associated with our diet. This mix of food, identity, and religion is evident in some of the hall-marks of Japanese cuisine.

Kami are deities in the Japanese religion, Shinto. Shown proper re-spect and gratitude, kami in turn bestow blessings and protection on sup-plicants. The most popular Shinto kami is Inari, widely venerated as a god of prosperity. Because messengers of Inari are foxes and foxes are said to be fond of tofu, it is common to offer aburage (fried tofu), at Inari shrines. Such offerings ensure the fox messengers will carry prayers to Inari and boons be granted as a result. Due to this association between foxes, abu-rage, and the kami of prosperity, cone sushi are called Inari sushi. Like-wise, the type of udon or soba noodles served at restaurants with pieces of aburage in the broth is called kitsune udon/soba (fox noodles).

There is also an earthy side to Japanese religion as kami may exhibit a bawdy sense of humor and the capacity for mischief. Kappa are impish be-ings that dwell in lakes and rivers. They are known for pulling unsuspect-ing swimmers below the surface, flipping them upside down, and sucking the blood from the helpless victim's anus. Kappa like to have fun. Kappa are said to be fond of cucumbers, however, and can be appeased by them instead. When swimming in a lake, therefore, it may be wise to stuff a cu-cumber in your pocket in the event that a kappa pulls you under the water. Eyeing your pocket, the kappa will be distracted and may wonder if there's a cucumber there or if you are simply happy to meet him. Regardless, the kappa will let you go and give full attention to the cucumber instead. Be-cause of their fondness for cucumbers, cucumber sushi is named in their honor and called kappa maki.

Shinto is filled with eight million kami, but despite the diversity, cer-tain themes or values characterize the religion. Four in particular are noteworthy: simplicity, respect for nature, purity, and gratitude.

These themes or values in Shinto permeate Japanese cuisine. In con-trast to the thinking of other cultures, where cooking is the art of trans-forming ingredients that are not yet edible into something delicious, and the creation of tastes that do not occur naturally, the traditional approach to Japanese cuisine emphasizes that food be enjoyed as close as possible to its natural state. In Japanese cuisine, the ideal way of cooking is not to cook. The perfect example of this is sashimi. Sashimi uses no heat whatsoever and consists of little more than slicing fresh fish and arranging its pieces on a plate. Sashimi conveys the Japanese values of simplicity, purity, and reverence for things in their natural state. As a result, sashimi is often the most expensive item on a Japanese restaurant menu. Ramen, by contrast, is usually the cheapest dish on a Japanese menu because it contains little (if any at all) of the aforementioned values. Regardless of what one eats, however, it is customary in Japanese tradition to begin and end meals with a set expression of gratitude.

If we define ourselves in part by the food we eat, we define our relationships in part by the meals we share. The emphasis on purity and the avoidance of pollution in Japanese religion underscores a number of table manners and eating habits.

Japanese chopsticks are usually made of plain, unpainted wood. Chopsticks are not shared and even the most expensive Japanese restaurants will provide a pair of unused, disposable wooden chopsticks for each customer. One's chopsticks are only allowed to touch one's personal serving of food and food is never passed directly from one pair of chopsticks to another. Moreover teishoku, or set meals, are often served in individual trays, where small compartments keep the different food items separate to prevent mixing and pollution. This is in stark contrast to the foods and eating habits of other religious and cultural traditions—the Chinese religion Daoism, for example—that stress the balance and harmony of different food combinations and the sharing of dishes by everyone at the table.

Food and eating habits are not determined simply by recipe and hunger, but by the traditions—religious and cultural—and the meanings associated with them. We are shaped by and shapers of food, culture, and religion. We preserve and perpetuate traditional flavors and recipes that reflect our ethnic and religious identities. Cooking and consuming such foods maintain and affirm our place in the wider cultural and religious community. In short, you are what you eat and you eat who you are.

Religion Rebel

The Sports Gods

The gods love sports. They are avid sports fans, judging from what goes on at sporting events. They watch and listen to the games and matches, or at least that is what they must be doing, if one goes by the words and deeds of the players, coaches, and fans. Prayers are said to invoke and thank the gods. Curses are offered in their names. Winners point to the sky and give public praise to their gods; losers search in private for consolation from theirs.

But the gods should not play games or take sides in sports, especially in youth sports. Indeed, it might be best if religion was not a part of school sports altogether, in particular contests that match the local private schools against public ones, as it gives yet another advantage to the ILH over the OIA. The private schools can pray to their gods for help; the public schools are prohibited from doing so. This is not fair. It is difficult to compete against god, or a team with god on its side. It is even more unfair when one team has a saint for it as well. It thus says something about the athletic program—or the power of god—if, even with god on the other side, the public schools still win.

Moreover, not all the gods are good for sports. Some are less competitive than others and do not demand suffering and a sacrificial death to achieve ultimate victory. Followers of such gods don't have scriptures readily available that celebrate or condone holy war. In short, Buddhist schools are at a disadvantage. It's hard to want to win when one is supposed to be selfless and giving. It is difficult for Buddhist athletes to attack and destroy the defenses of their opponents when they are supposed to practice compassion. This must be the explanation behind those committing costly game errors that result in victory for the other side—they were secretly practicing Buddhism. Even in defeat, however, there is the solace of spiritual victory—moral lessons learned, strength of character earned—available to comfort those who fall short in the world of sports.

Real victory, though, may come when the gods are not asked to help score points or be present at games or give their blessings to opening day festivities for little league baseball, but when all those involved in sports ask the gods to turn away from the games and turn their attention instead to help the less fortunate in the world and those suffering from unspeakable horrors. Can't the gods do both, some may wonder? Apparently not, if what is reported in the news is any indication. Yet the faithful know tragedy and disaster do not diminish the grandeur of their gods, but serve to strengthen their own resolve to do good in the world and to resist despair and defeat. This is the competitor spirit revealed in sports. Whether this spirit carries the athlete to an immediate sports victory or to a greater achievement much later in life, only the gods know. The gods may take the credit for such victories. If not, their players are often glad to do so for them instead.

The Disease
And Cure Of Religion

I am the wrong kind of doctor. I am the poor kind. I have a PhD, but it's not in a lucrative field—it's in religion. And though I love what I do, I can't perform surgery or prescribe amoxicillin. When I am sick, I can offer numerous prayers for healing but they don't work—the gods don't respond to me. Doesn't matter, when I'm not feeling well I make an appointment to visit the right kind of doctor—a medical doctor.

Over the years of medical doctor visits, I've learned that when someone in the family has a bad cough, sore throat and headache, one of the first things we must do before deciding on a course of action is to determine whether the cause of the illness is a bacterial infection or a viral infection, as treatment for the two will differ. Bacterial infections can be treated with antibiotics. If it's a viral infection, however, we can treat its symptoms to help us feel better, but there's usually no effective medication for a viral infection. The best medicine is prevention.

Religious belief is like an infection.

Although I can't help anyone suffering from bronchitis or influenza A, I can help my students and family resist something that poses a dangerous threat to our well-being nonetheless—religious extremism. Religion can be good overall, but some believe there is only one religious truth and that those who do not share their narrow views will be condemned to eternal suffering. Such believers are infected by a blinding faith and can easily succumb to religious extremism.

Religious extremism is often cultivated and spread among those with little or no prior knowledge or understanding of religion. Those who grew up with a moderate form religion are on the whole not contagious. It's the religious convert we must be wary of. Therefore, if we think of religious extremism as a disease—an infection of the mind that impedes our ability to think and use common sense —we may look to the usual methods to treat or limit the spread of infectious diseases: antibiotics and vaccination.

For the spiritual health of my students and family, I administer religious antibiotics and faith vaccinations. I give students prescribed doses of the different world religions to help them fight off religious intolerance and vaccinate my family by exposing them to moderate strains of faith traditions in order to develop a level of immunity to religious fanaticism.

While my family has a church that we belong to, on alternate weeks my wife and I drag our children to other places of worship—different churches, temples, synagogues, mosques, shrines—to expose them to the wide range of religious beliefs and practices found on the island. We do the same when traveling abroad. Most of the time we make great choices. Our weekly sojourns to our home church and other places of worship have given us opportunities to cultivate meaningful experiences and meet wonderful people and communities of faith. Other times our visits are unpleasant—not as painful as a flu shot, but uncomfortable nonetheless. Through all of this, we learn to appreciate and respect the different religions. Our children see for themselves the good (and strange) in each tradition. After every visit we discuss what we liked and didn't like about the religious service. By introducing moderate forms of religion, we lessen the chance of our children being infected by religious extremism.

Most bacteria are harmless and some are even good, living in our intestines and helping us digest our food. Religious faith can be like bacteria, helping us digest the ups and downs of life. However, there are many infectious diseases out there that we should be mindful of. Religious extremism is an infectious disease. But so is love. And judging by last week's Valentine's Day activities, there is no doctor with an effective cure or vaccination for that.

Religion Awards

If there were religious equivalents to the Oscar or Grammy awards, Jesus would win the award for "Most Likely To Be Crucified." The Buddha would win for "Most Likely To Rest Under A Tree," Muhammad for "Most Revelations Received From God By One Man," and Moses for "Most Likely To Be Replaced By A Golden Calf." And after they finished thanking God for their awards, the religious greats would undoubtedly acknowledge the women who made everything possible.

The crucifixion of Christ, the enlightenment of the Buddha, the revelations to Muhammad, and the call to Moses on Mt. Sinai no longer have the same appeal to me, as fantastic as they are. Perhaps it's because I've heard and read the stories so many times and studied the tales for so long that I take them for granted. What I find more poignant are the stories of the women who were left behind or who gave of themselves to allow the men to reach their religious goals.

While the canonical gospels of Matthew, Mark, and Luke tell us that the disciples of Jesus (and apparently God too) had forsaken him at the cross, Mary Magdalene did not leave him. Non-biblical traditions state that she and Jesus shared an intimate relationship. The non-canonical *Gospel of Mary* and *Gospel of Philip*, for example, explicitly state that Jesus loved Mary more than the other disciples. Even the New Testament writings provide hints that she and Jesus had a special bond. She is the only one mentioned in all four gospels to have been at the cross when the other disciples had abandoned Jesus, and she was the first person to find Jesus' tomb empty. Standing outside the empty tomb and crying, Mary said, "They have taken my Lord away and I don't know where they have laid him." Thinking a gardener had moved the body, Mary said to him: "Sir, if you have carried him away, tell me where you have laid him, and I will take him." When Mary realized that the gardener was Jesus, she cried out to him but Jesus told her, "Do not hold on to me, because I have not yet ascended to the Father." Instead, she is directed to tell the disciples what she had experienced—the risen Christ. Mary was the first one to whom the risen Christ appeared and was the first one entrusted with the responsibility of sharing the good news with others. One wonders about the development of Christianity had Mary not gone to the tomb and discovered it empty.

While others criticized and attacked (verbally and physically) the prophet of God, Khadija was the first to give unconditional support to her husband, Muhammad.

Muhammad said about his wife Khadija: "She believed in me when no one else did; she accepted Islam when people rejected me; and she helped and comforted me when there was no one else to lend me a helping hand." Khadija was the first to believe in Islam and used all her resources (she was a successful business woman) to help and protect the faithful who were persecuted, many of whom were poor and without much social or political power. While Khadija was alive she was Muhammad's only wife and even after she died, whenever gifts were sent to Muhammad, he set aside a portion of the gifts to give to Khadija's friends as a way to honor his wife. Khadija was not kept hidden behind a veil of secrecy, but was at the forefront of Islam as its first believer.

Moses was a reluctant servant of God and God intended to kill Moses on his way back to Egypt. But Moses' wife Zipporah saved him. While Moses was a newcomer in his relationship with God, Zipporah was already familiar with the deity of the burning bush and knew what God wanted (her father was a priest). At the lodging where God intended to kill Moses, Zipporah took a knife, cut off her son's foreskin, and touched Moses' "feet" (perhaps a euphemism for penis) with the bloody prepuce, and God let him alone. For all her quick thinking and bravery, however, tradition says Moses did not love her, and she was returned to her father's house. She was brought back to Moses after the exodus from Egypt. While Moses tried to avoid the task God had designed for him, Zipporah understood what God wanted and acted, saving her husband from death as a result. Without Moses, the story of Jews, Christians, and Muslims would be quite different.

When Yasodhara, the former wife of the Buddha, had a premonition that her husband would leave her behind in pursuit of his religious quest, she asked him for a promise that he would take her with him. When she awoke one morning and found that her husband had left during the course of the night, she emulated his spiritual practices in hopes that he would return for her. She shaved the hair off of her head just as he had, she donned the robes of a mendicant as he had, she subjected herself to extreme fasting as he did, and slept on the hard ground as he was wont to do. She cried everyday because despite all that she did, her husband did not return. People around her spread rumors that Yasodhara's husband abandoned her because she was an unfit wife and mother. Yasodhara grieved and longed for her husband. She was lonely and angry, but she still worried about him for six years (what he would eat, where he would sleep, and who would care for him). Other suitors came to ask for her hand in marriage, but she replied that she still belonged to her husband. When Yasodhara's husband finally returned six years later, he was no longer an ordinary man. He was the Buddha. He praised Yasodhara's faith and her sacrifice and patience that allowed him to achieve enlightenment, and she too reached spiritual liberation. Though in separate fashions they had indeed embarked on their religious paths together.

Despite the vital importance of women for the historical foundation of each of the religions mentioned above, today they are mostly denied equal leadership roles with the men of their faith. A simple look at the churches, temples, mosques, shrines, and synagogues on the island demonstrates this. It is an affront to the founders of the great religions—who turned to and trusted women—that the majority of their present day followers cannot bring themselves to do the same and acknowledge women leaders as senior pastor, priest, rabbi, imam, or minister at their places of worship. What does it say about the integrity and development of religious faiths that though women played instrumental roles in the success of their religions, men dominate the leadership positions and the only recognition women receive is "Best Supporting Role"?

Christians At
Buddhist Funerals

I am on the whole reluctant to give personal advice to readers and students regarding how they should go about practicing their religion. I do my best to explain the scholarly point of view concerning religion, but I am not comfortable with questions that seek guidance regarding private matters of faith. In my view, as long as one's religion does not promote intolerance or hate and does not hurt anyone, be as religious or unreligious as you want to be.

But perhaps it is due to the summer-long Bon Dance season—when Buddhist temples and practices garner public attention because of Obon-related festivities—that I tend to receive more questions from Christians about how to behave at Buddhist services during this time of the year.

A common question I receive is similar to this one:

"My husband and I are Christians, but my husband's family is not. They are Buddhists. There is a Buddhist funeral coming up and we of course will have to attend. During the service, we will be asked to come forward, bow, put our hands together in prayer

*and offer incense to the deceased and the Buddha. What should
we do? We don't want to be disrespectful to the family, but we are
devout Christians."*

My response? The answer is complex yet simple.

Complicated because the answer to the question largely depends on
the attitude and intention of the one performing the gesture at the Buddhist funeral. In general, pressing one's palms together and bowing in
Buddhism does not have the same meaning as it does in Christianity. Putting one's hands together in the Buddhist tradition (gassho) is not a form
of worship or prayer to the dead. It is a form of etiquette meant to convey
respect and gratitude.

Buddhists place their palms together as a symbol of the unity of opposites or complements: oneself and others, past and present, life and death,
the sacred and the ordinary. In other words, opposites are really one. In
Buddhism, placing the palms together expresses the inter-connectedness
we share with each other and the gratitude that arises from this realization.

As such, Buddhists will often greet each other by placing their hands
together and bowing. They are not praying to each other or worshiping
one another. In a sense, it is the Buddhist equivalent of a hug or handshake. Not understanding this can lead to awkward situations and unnecessary strains in relationships. For example, I know some people who
don't allow their children to participate in the martial arts because they
mistakenly think bowing in the dojo and before matches in a tournament
is a form of idolatry. I've also witnessed the strange scenario where one
person bowed while the other person reciprocated by extending a hand
for a handshake instead.

Understanding the cultural context of a gesture is important. The shaka sign, for example, can mean different things in different places. Making
shaka too close to your face—where the little finger is near your mouth
and the thumb near your ear—is a gesture for having a telephone conversation. In China, the shaka sign is the gesture for the number 6. The gesture is also the sign for the letter "Y" in the American Manual Alphabet.

Complicating matters further, placing one's palms together is not a required or inherent act for prayer even among people who worship the same God. Jews and Muslims, for example, don't put their hands together when praying, even though they worship the same God that Christians do. Why, then, do Christians traditionally place their palms together and kneel in prayer? While the origin of the prayer gesture is not clear and there are several possibilities, the act is associated with notions of subjugation and control. The Apostle Paul says, Christians were once slaves to sin; but are now slaves to righteousness through Jesus Christ. To express this, Christians kneel with their hands symbolically bound together.

Long story short, there are Christians in my family and among my friends who bow, offer incense and place their hands together at Buddhist funerals to show respect and gratitude to the deceased. The family of the deceased is deeply appreciative when this occurs. There are also Christians among my family and friends who refuse to go up to the altar area and offer incense at Buddhist funerals. I don't blame them because I understand their misunderstanding, but others view them in a negative light, especially those who hold the stereotypical view of Christians as intolerant and narrow-minded.

Simply put, for Christians at a Buddhist funeral it ultimately comes down to this: what's more important—the feelings of the family who belongs to the Buddhist tradition who have lost a loved one, or one's own personal faith? Do you worship a God loving enough who would look kindly on a person who shows compassion for others, even if it means participating in a religious tradition different from one's own? Or would your God cast you away for such acts of kindness?

Heaven Is A Place On Earth

I probably have the worst job when it comes to making small talk with people. I teach religion courses at Leeward Community College and UH Mānoa, but I don't want people I've just met to know this. It will often make for a long, uncomfortable conversation otherwise.

However, all too often I have to contact a company for help with home, yard, or auto repair. I try to avoid working with businesses that use a fish symbol in its advertisement because I dread the five words: "So, what do you do?"

Sometimes I have no choice but to respond, especially when getting contract work estimates. Here are the first five questions a work estimator asked me after finding out I was a religion professor: "Do you tell your students that Christ is the only way?" "Really?" "Don't you know what the Bible says?" "Aren't you worried about misleading your students and sending them to hell?" "What makes you think hell has better music?"

When one thinks about it, what is so great about heaven? I don't need 72 virgins and I don't know how to play the harp. I'd be bored. I suppose it depends on the concept of heaven.

When I asked the question, "Why go to heaven?" the work estimator told me to imagine the happiest time in my life. "Multiply that by a million and you get close to what heaven is like." Nice. But some of the people dearest to me won't be there (or so I'm told) because they had the unfortunate luck to be born in the wrong culture and raised in the wrong religion as a result. This makes me sad. Now multiply that by a million and see how happy one can be. What is more, those who had a faith conversion before their deaths, such as serial rapists and killers like Jeffrey Dahmer or Ted Bundy, get eternal life in heaven by the sheer luck of being born and raised in the United States where Christianity is the dominant religion. Think of spending eternity with Jeff and Ted. Now times that by a million. No thanks. This is what French philosopher Jean-Paul Sartre must have had in mind when he said hell is other people.

I would rather spend eternity with decent people of any faith or of no faith at all, than with religiously converted killers and rapists. I'm guessing their victims might feel similarly.

The concept of an eternal afterlife in heaven is not found in the earliest books of the Bible (the Torah or Pentateuch), however. It was incorporated into the scriptural tradition many centuries later. In the earliest biblical traditions, the emphasis was on this world. Rewards and punishments were meted out here. The Quran echoes this too (surah 29:27). For example, the eternal covenant God made with Abraham did not include a promise of eternity in heaven, but the promise of land and children—in this world. This explains the strong emphasis on producing children in stories of the Bible e.g., Abraham and Sarah, Isaac and Rebekah, Jacob and Rachel. From this perspective, eternal life meant living through one's children. (More specifically through one's sons, since they carried on the name. This explains the tradition of naming boys "Junior." There is no "Junior Girl.")

This version of an eternal life—where God rewards decent and faithful people with the promise of a prosperous family who will carry on after the parents are gone—is preferable to me than the one inhabited by serial killers and rapists who converted to avoid hell, or by bigots and racists who are rewarded with heavenly bliss simply because they confessed faith in God, despite their hateful views.

There is a nice story of the difference between heaven and hell that I first heard in the Buddhist tradition, but is found in several other religious traditions too. In hell, there is wonderful food and drink spread out lavishly across a table, but those suffering in hell are starving because they can't eat. Why not? In hell, people have no elbows so they are unable bring the food or drink to their mouths. In heaven, by contrast, there is also a table with food and drink, and the people there also don't have elbows. But they are perfectly happy and well fed. They feed each other.

I also offered another interpretation of heaven I like based on a Jewish tradition. In heaven we sit in a large classroom and listen to a lecture and take notes for all eternity. For my students, this may seem more like hell than heaven, but the difference is this: the one giving the lecture is not a sexy, 5' 7" tall, 180 lbs., 50 year-old Japanese-American male. It's God. What is more, we get to ask God any and all questions and we will receive all the answers.

But the contract estimator would have none of this and—despite my attempts to end the conversation—proceeded to torment me with his point of view for the next 45 minutes. Sartre was right. It is at those times I wish I had a job that made people uncomfortable or a little self-conscious about opening their mouths. At those times I wish I were a dentist instead.

To Hell And Back

It's not easy to go to hell. There are no direct flights from Hawaiʻi and the journey will take anywhere from 23 to 40 hours. It's about 9,000 miles from paradise to hell.

The term that the Bible translates as "hell" is *Gehenna*. Gehenna is an actual geographical place on earth—a valley south of Jerusalem. The name Gehenna is derived from "Valley of the Son(s) of Hinnom." In turn, "Son(s) of Hinnom" was the biblical designation for an ancient Canaanite group that occupied the land area before King David was said to have captured Jerusalem, around 1,000 BCE.

During biblical times, Gehenna was associated with idol worship and gained a vile reputation as a place of forbidden religious practices. Gehenna was the site of child sacrifices and where biblical kings burned humans as offerings to the gods. In the Hebrew Bible (Old Testament in Christianity), Gehenna was a real place where people were put to death; not an imaginary world where people went to after they died.

Instead, Sheol was commonly referred to in the Bible as the place where the departed spirits traveled to after death. Sheol was often thought of as a gloomy and murky region in the underworld where everyone—righteous and unrighteous alike—dwelled in a shadowy existence. Although Sheol was considered bleak and dark, it was not a land of torment for the sinful. Sheol was often simply used to talk about a place that held all of the dead.

However, as the biblical writers came into contact with other religious and cultural traditions and were exposed to different ideas about anguish and suffering in the afterlife, Gehenna became a symbol of God's punishment and a place of torture for the wicked. Gehenna was transformed into a realm of burning destruction for those who led corrupt lives. Indeed, in 1 Enoch and other books written during the time between the Hebrew Bible and the New Testament, Gehenna is associated with fire, judgment, and eternal damnation. By the time the New Testament was written, ideas about Gehenna as a fiery place of punishment and torture had been developed and incorporated into the worldview of the biblical writers.

In short, because of its associations with fiery destruction and judgment, Gehenna was no longer viewed as an actual physical spot on earth, but came to be used metaphorically as a designation for hell or eternal damnation. This is how Jesus used the term—as a reference to a place of posthumous torment and not as a geographic place name.

However, even in the words of Jesus, one's fate in the afterlife was determined by one's action rather than a confession of faith. Jesus says this clearly in the Gospel of Matthew: "Not everyone who says to me, 'Lord, Lord', will enter the kingdom of heaven, but only the one who does the will of my Father in heaven." (Matthew 7:21)

Instead, not showing care and compassion for the social outcast or for those who were disadvantaged would get you sent to hell: "Then he (Son of Man) will say to those at his left hand, 'You that are accursed, depart from me into the eternal fire prepared for the devil and his angels; for I was hungry and you gave me no food, I was thirsty and you gave me nothing to drink, I was a stranger and you did not welcome me, naked and you did not give me clothing, sick and in prison and you did not visit me.'" (Matthew 25:41-43)

Today, there are travel tours to Jerusalem that include side trips to Gehenna. One can even find sightseeing reviews by those who have gone to hell and back. And based on these reviews, it seems hell is quite mundane.

No orgies, devils, or heavy metal music. In fact, it appears many of the tourists who visit Hinnom Valley are the religiously devout. This seems appropriate.

The average daily temperature in Gehenna in January is in the 50s, which means Hawai'i is hotter than hell. But it's not too early to think about summer travel plans. A roundtrip air ticket to Gehenna may cost about $1500. But there is a cheaper and easier way to get to hell. Talk to some of the religious people who try to convert you to their faith. They believe their god sends certain groups of people to hell for free.

Religion & Education

In the religion department at UH Mānoa, we have t-shirts that say, "Sin is Our Business."

But sin—wherever it is and in whatever form it takes, whether real or imagined—is also apparently good for business, as it steers parents towards enrolling their children in increasingly popular religious-based schools. Perhaps too, it is the sinful temptation of good-looking professors behind the popularity of religion courses at college campuses across the UH system. Perhaps it is not. Yet sin is everywhere for those who look for it, even if it's only in the mind. And this form of sin can ruin everything, even the joy of fourth graders on a school trip to the Big Island. A religion teacher at one of the local private schools wished her excited students a fun trip, but in the same breath warned them against believing in the Hawaiian gods and in their stories while there. Such episodes would be amusing if they also weren't commonplace. Instead, they are sad and deeply disturbing.

Teaching children to be intolerant of other faiths (even of different versions of the same one)—and by extension of other cultures—is wrong. It borders on child abuse. Children subjected to such forms of religious education grow up wary of other religions, other cultures, other people and, indeed the world. This view is quite different from the perspective of healthy children. Instead of being encouraged to ask questions and think for themselves, to be open-minded and appreciative of diversity, they are told repeatedly that all the necessary answers for understanding life lie in the deciphering of ancient texts, and when present-day realities of the world contradict these texts, the children are taught the world is wrong and should be rejected. Such a worldview may cause harm that is long lasting. What is more, children fortunate enough to escape from such a restrictive worldview may have trouble assimilating into the wider social culture not just because it was alien to them for so long, but because they have been taught that it was wicked and to be feared. For children still trapped in this frightening worldview, Halloween is evil, celebrating Thanksgiving is wrong, bowing at martial arts practice is idol worshipping, learning hula is a form of pagan worship. These holidays and practices are not the insidious tentacles of sin, but wonderful expressions of diverse cultures and values that are held dear by many.

Teach children to be awe-inspired, not wary and afraid. Skepticism, inquiry, and doubt can be great tools to give learning children. With them children can build a worldview filled with wonder, beauty, and awe. In stark contrast, the absoluteness, intolerance, and fear of sin preached in some forms of religious education impede innovation, exploration, and discovery and therefore should have no place in an academic setting.

Yet the academic study of religion is important, and not all schools teach religion in such a narrow-minded, fearful way. Indeed, religion is the most important subject of study at college. This is not simply my opinion. More people love, hate, help, kill, and die (and write nasty emails) because of religion than for any other college subject of study. No one dies for Composition English. Nobody straps dynamite on their body, walks into a crowded market place, and blows herself up for Pre-Calculus Math. But for religion, people do incredible stuff, and incredibly stupid stuff. Through the study of religion, one is introduced to history, politics, science, art, and a host of other wonderful study subjects.

Religion therefore should be taught to elementary school children in the same way that culture is: with respect and appreciation for the similarities and differences, strengths and weaknesses, between various people living in different places and in different ways. Children should not be forced to believe that one is superior to the rest, and that the alternatives are dangerously wrong, even if their parents believe such nonsense. Imagine the uproar if all nine year olds were taught that Japanese culture is the best. This may or may not be true, but it shouldn't be taught. The study of religion opens up fascinating glimpses for students to see and determine for themselves the true and untrue. Sin does not. But sin is business and—judging by the weekly emails I receive—business is good.

Hawai'i Is Paradise

Hawai'i is paradise. At least it is when it comes to religion. Few places in the world can match Hawai'i in regards to the collection and variety of religions available in one location. Judaism, Christianity, Islam, Hinduism, Buddhism, Daoism, Shinto, Sikhism, Bahai and a host of smaller religious groups can be easily found in the islands. Hawai'i is a wonderful place to study and—more importantly—learn to respect and appreciate the diversity of religious cultures. There is enough intolerance in the world. Let's not tolerate intolerance here.

And yet there are religious groups that foster discrimination and prejudice among their followers towards other religions. I've personally heard ignorant and bigoted statements spewed by religious leaders and their followers at different places of worship—even at a funeral—so I know it's not just one religion or one particular place of worship that foments intolerance and prejudice.

There are many kindhearted and decent people in Hawai'i who would never think to denigrate a person's ethnicity or speak ill of a person's sexual orientation. They are wonderful people in every regard, except when it comes to religion.

They would not utter racist or sexist comments, but substitute religion for race and gender and suddenly it becomes acceptable to discriminate. Why is this? At their places of worship they learn that it is okay to demean other religious traditions as inferior at best and dangerous and evil at worst. I've heard people say things that make me wince, such as "Islam is evil" and "Buddhism is full of idol worshippers."

Islam and Buddhism are just as good—and as terrible—as any other religion. Visit a mosque or walk into a Buddhist temple and see. No religion has a monopoly on righteousness or corruption.

Education is the best way to combat ignorance and the fear and prejudice that accompany it.

To promote religious tolerance and understanding in my *World Religions* classes, I require students to visit five different religions. If it were a *Foods of the World* course, I'd have them eat at five different ethnic restaurants. Imagine how silly it would sound if a student complained about such an assignment, saying his parents only allow him to eat Chinese food, or he can't eat Italian food because it will turn him away from Hawaiian food. Think of how annoying it would be if a person claimed vegetarianism was the only way and that all meat-eaters are murderers. (Wait, we already have people like that!) Substitute Christianity for vegetarianism and Islam for beef (or vice versa) and you get the idea.

Even so, I've actually had a student tell me that she couldn't do the assignment because her church does not allow her to visit any other place of worship, not even another church! A few semesters later, another student told me that her Buddhist temple warned her of personal tragedies that she and her family would incur if she left her religion for another. I feel sorry for students raised in such religious settings.

If your place of worship denigrates others because of their ethnicity, religion, gender or sexual orientation; leave. If your place of worship is so insecure that it won't allow you to visit any other place of worship, get out while you still can. There are many fantastic churches, temples, and shrines that are welcoming and filled with wonderful people. They are easy to find.

What about those who claim that their discriminatory views are firmly rooted in scripture? Yes, it's not difficult to find scriptural passages that give legitimacy to prejudice. However, one also can easily find scriptural support in the same books for the opposite, more accepting point of view. It's our choice to see what we want to see.

Everyone is aware that a balanced lifestyle is healthy. Likewise, a well rounded education for our children should include (among other things) a blend of science, art, physical education, music, literature, math, recess and lunch. This should apply to religion too. Why limit yourself to one place of worship? We don't perform only one kind of exercise, eat only one kind of food, or study just one subject at school.

We may have only one spouse, but meeting up with friends or engaging in activities apart from our spouse is healthy for the relationship as a whole. Similarly, my family has a home church. Yet on alternate weeks we visit other places of worship. This is healthy for us. We see the good (and strange) in each tradition. We learn to appreciate and respect (and critique) the different religions.

In this day and age of religious extremism, denying oneself an education in religion is a form of live burial. It leads to spiritual death and—as the atrocities committed in the name of religion make clear—other kinds of death as well. There are religious bigots whose only goal is paradise. Let's not turn Hawai'i into that kind of paradise.

Conclusion &
Remembrance

The day I dreaded ever since I was a little boy arrived in the late afternoon on February 23, 2016. My mom died. The next day was my birthday and for the very first time in my life, Barbara Jean Sakashita was not there to wish me "happy birthday" as she had done every other year of my life. I miss my mom's love.

A mother loves unconditionally and will place the needs of her children before her own. A mother does not demand that her children worship her or sacrifice themselves to make amends, no matter how they may have disappointed her. Perhaps for these reasons I turned to my mom instead of God more times than not during the lowest moments in my life.

My mom was my first religion teacher, though not a very good one. She was a staunch Episcopalian, but she couldn't explain what that meant. And while she tried to teach me to appreciate sincerity instead of status; effort instead of accolades; and love and forgiveness instead of self-righteousness and pride; to her chagrin, my behavior often times did not reflect those values. But she loved me nonetheless. And she embodied the ideals of the Episcopal Church in her own way: she examined her religion critically and could disagree with its teachings when she felt it was necessary. She could also laugh with and love people who didn't belong to her religion or to any religion at all. In fact, my mom married my dad, whose family belonged to the Soto Zen Buddhist tradition. Luckily, the Episcopal Church teaches, "God loves you. No exceptions." Love—divine and otherwise—transcends categories and boundaries, no matter the attempts by some to regulate or control whom we love. My parents were married at St. Andrew's Cathedral—an Episcopal church. Her funeral was there too. I also married a Buddhist and we had our wedding in Scotland, at a church formerly called, St. Andrew's. Though my mom and I were the two Christians in a family of five, truth be told, the non-Christians in the family reflected mom's values better than I ever did. I hope my children follow in their ways.

It is difficult watching your mother die. It's difficult to see the woman who gave you life lose hers. During my mom's last days I sat at her bedside, trying to align my breath with hers. I imagined that if I synchronized our breathing, I could somehow give her some of my strength so that her body didn't have to fight the illness by itself.

How could God allow good people to suffer? Why would God take any mother away from her children? Such questions used to cause me deep anguish, but no longer because the answer (if there is one) doesn't matter. I've forgiven God instead. My mom was different. Throughout her illness, my mom was not angry with God. She did not abandon God. Her love remained unconditional.

My mom lived for 76 years. But the quality of life is not simply determined by its length, but by its width and depth—and by the people we love. By these criteria she had a good life. When she could still talk, I asked her to tell me what was best about her life. She said there were so many things, but when I pressed her to name just one, she said, "Your dad. He is so good to me." My mom is no longer here to teach me, but I continue to learn from my dad.

I still have conversations with my mom as I walk to and from my religion classes. I tell her how we are trying to cope with life without her. I tell her how lonely I feel. I tell her about her grandchildren, and when I do this, I am filled with happiness and sadness at the same time—happy thinking about how much they loved each other and the good times they shared; but sad knowing such good times will never occur again. There are days when I want to cancel my classes, but I don't because my mom was a dedicated elementary school teacher. And while she is not here anymore, I still try to make her proud of me.

The love of a mother for her child is not bound to any particular faith or religion. It transcends anything and everything. A mother's love is not even limited to life itself. It can find its way through the dark moments of emptiness and sorrow and reach a grieving son who has lost his mom.

By the time this comes to print, Mother's Day will have passed. (My mom also tried to teach me not to procrastinate.) Still, I want to wish all mothers a belated "Happy Mother's Day" just the same. And though I know my mom will never again read my *MidWeek* column, I want to extend the sentiment to her as well. "Happy Mother's Day, Mom." I miss you very much.

About the Author

An alumnus of the University of Hawai'i, Sakashita received his Ph.D. degree from the University of Stirling in Scotland, where his research focused on contemporary Japanese religions. His work has appeared in newspapers, magazines, journals, and books.

Sakashita is Professor of Religion at Leeward Community College and a lecturer at UH Mānoa, where he teaches various religion courses, including those related to Christianity and Japanese religions.

Sakashita also writes a column on religion in the *MidWeek* newspaper called, "Misfit Spirit." He has no hobbies, no time to read books, and absolutely no social life. This is his children's fault.